I Hate to Be Late!

I Hate to Be Late!

Great Strategies to
Help You Be On Time

By
Leslie Ann Cardinal

The Cardinal Success Books Series

Disclaimer

The opinions expressed in this book are not a guarantee of results, because your results are determined by your own efforts and decisions. The ideas and opinions in this book are not meant to take the place of legal, tax, medical or other professional advice. If you need advice, please seek the help of a qualified professional.

© Copyright 2015 by Leslie Ann Cardinal
Hunter's Moon Publishing
ISBN: 978-1-937988-19-7

Thank you for purchasing this book!

I am excited to bring resources to help you achieve professional and personal success.

I have some special free resources to help you in your quest to be on time. To receive them, go to

http://IHateToBeLate.com

I am excited to hear about your successes with being on time!

Dedication

This book is dedicated to my great friend and colleague, the late Jim Symcox. Jim was committed to excellence and he was always willing to help and encourage the people around him. Jim was full of wisdom and had a caring heart. We first met at the Park Hills Career Transition Ministry, where we taught and coached people to find their next successful career steps. We went on to work together on a variety of other business projects to help individuals and organizations to build team cohesiveness, strong leadership skills, and the communications and interpersonal skills needed to achieve outstanding business success. Thank you for being a wonderful inspiration!

Table of Contents

Foreword

by Connie Ragen Green

When Leslie Cardinal first asked me if I would write a Foreword for her new book, my initial thought was that I wouldn't have enough time to get it to her quickly enough to meet her deadline. Funny how time plays such a crucial role in many of our life decisions, isn't it? We all seem to live by the clock, and the result is sometimes not what we had hoped for.

I first met Leslie online many years ago. It was her professional manner and kind demeanor that first got my attention. Soon she was a regular part of my teleseminars and webinars and I could see that she very intelligent and gave great attention to details. I was in awe of her ability to move seamlessly between the online and offline worlds, and when she told me she had come from a corporate background I could understand more about how she was able to maneuver through the complexities of situations I remained clueless about.

We finally met in person in Austin, Texas in 2009. I was attending a Mastermind Retreat with a group I had been a part of for about a year, and Leslie drove up from San Antonio to meet me for lunch. We hit it off immediately, and this was the beginning of what I consider to be a very special friendship and business relationship we continue to nurture and expand.

Leslie has become something of an expert in the area of time and time management. In our entrepreneurial world of fast-paced actions and superficial implementation, she has made a thorough study of why people are late and how to remedy that situation. Instead of just proceeding through her life not knowing the answers to these and other pertinent questions, Leslie is always researching, experimenting, and asking the tough questions no one else is willing to ask in order to solve this age old problem.

Your life will be enriched by connecting with Leslie Cardinal. She is unique in that she doesn't so much worry about what others think as she does about how they will succeed with their life's goals. I find this to be a unique and refreshing perspective and wish I had had the courage to go for this philosophy much earlier in my own life. I have watched her over the years go one step further than anyone else I know to make sure those around her have exactly what they need. She has been like a sister to me at times and a mentor at others, all the while showing care and concern over what was truly important to me. She'll do the same for you if you allow her into your world.

Read this book with an open mind and an open heart. The thoughts, ideas, and opinions expressed here are the result of many years of experience. Sometimes the most difficult topics can be broken down into bite sized chunks in order to explore the possibilities, and that is what Leslie has done with this format. Be open to thinking about time, tardiness, and punctuality in an entirely new way and you'll be setting yourself up for great success.

Connie Ragen Green
Santa Barbara, California
http://ConnieRagenGreen.com

Foreword

by Cynthia Charleen Alexander

When I think about Leslie Cardinal, the first thing that comes to mind is the words "Grace and Poise." She always knows the right thing to say or do. When I need to know what to do or say, I channel my inner "Leslie" and think of what she would suggest. It never fails me.

We first became friends through our mentor Connie Ragen Green. I asked Connie to suggest a roommate when I was going to a marketing event. Leslie was a perfect match and we have become good friends as well as colleagues. We are so different in some ways: I feel dressed up when I put on good clothes and makeup while Leslie does hair, jewelry and classy outfits on a daily basis. I sit at the front of the conference room, while Leslie sits toward the back so she can meet and greet persons of interest and learn about their business ideas.

However, we have common ground and a shared interest in learning how to establish and grow a successful business. Leslie has a background in engineering and a Master's degree in Adult Education. It is these gifts for logical thinking and educational design that enables her to ask the right questions and bring out the interests and talents in the people that she meets.

I have had the privilege of hearing the passion she brings to her work as a business and leadership coach. She loves to see her clients make strong progress toward their goals, whether it is to advance in their careers or to grow their businesses. Leslie works with them to uncover their unique talents and skills and then coaches them to utilize these qualities to achieve their goals. Being of service by helping people to succeed is Leslie's mission and purpose in life.

I have also been in groups where Leslie asks the right questions and guides the group so that all are included in the decision. She shares her insights and inspiration in subtle, but effective ways. She always strives to draw everyone into the conversation.

If there is a theme to working with Leslie, it is her "you can do it, too" attitude. When a colleague is in crisis, Leslie knows the right thing to say and do. If you are looking for practical and DO-able advice, she is the person to talk with. Time and time again, Leslie goes beyond the expectations of the people she talks with to help them find solutions. Her level of caring abounds.

I was excited when I learned that Leslie was writing a book about being on time, a topic that is an issue for so many people. Whether in a business or relationship, being on time is so important. In this book, she has shared ways that she manages her time and she has asked for the tips and experiences of others so that you receive great value. Every chapter will give you helpful strategies and encouragement.

If you want to learn to be on time, this book has a wealth of valuable information that she has gathered by asking the right people the right questions. You can use this information to make changes, if you need to, or to make being punctual a continuing practice. What a great resource! Dive in, find your nuggets of inspiration, receive the gift of time and efficiency and reap the rewards!

Thank you, Leslie, for taking time to help so many by writing on this topic!

Cynthia Charleen Alexander
Professional Organizer
April 2015

Introduction

I was flying home from a conference, working on this book during the flight. The man next to me asked me what the book was about. I told him it would be about strategies for helping people to be on time and to not be late. He looked at me and smiled and said, "That will be a short book." When I asked him what he meant, he said, "Just tell them to get a watch!"

In fact, when I told my friends that I was writing a book about being on time, most of them chuckled or even laughed out loud, and I had to laugh with them. They knew that I had challenges with being on time and they were surprised that I of all people would write a book on this topic.

I Hate To Be Late

The truth is, I really hate to be late! It is so uncomfortable, and even embarrassing, to be late. And I hate to inconvenience people by making them wait. It is stressful and frustrating to everyone. Being late is hard on health and relationships and careers.

I started this book project with a personal goal: to get better about being on time. I wanted to see if I could find practical strategies and techniques that I could use in my everyday life to enable me to be on time. I wanted to share the things that I learned so I could help other people who struggle with being late too.

This book is part of the Cardinal Success Books Series. The goal of these books is to help you achieve new levels of success in your professional and personal life. These books are filled with practical ideas that you can put to use right away in your life. As a business and career coach I am always on the lookout for great ideas and resources to help my clients reach their goals quickly and with ease and joy. Now, with these books I can share them with you so that you can reap the benefits too.

Being On Time Has Always Been a Challenge

Struggling to be on time is something that has been a challenge for me for most of my life. Whether it was getting to class or to work, arriving at meetings, or getting together with friends or family for dinner, I had trouble being consistently on time. It was hard on my self esteem, hard on my relationships, and it just wasn't how I wanted to be in my personal and professional life.

The prevailing attitude among people who are naturally on time seems to be that they tend to believe that it should be an easy thing to be on time. They often attribute very negative character flaws to people who are late. They think that people who are late are rude or inconsiderate or worse. It can cause arguments, hurt relationships, reduce business productivity, and even ruin friendships.

At the beginning of 2014, I set a New Year's resolution to be more on time. To try to accomplish this goal, I looked in the traditional places like books and websites and time management classes to try to find ideas and techniques. Most of these resources just tell you to be early, or to not be late. Unfortunately, I found very little information about how to actually be on time.

Tapping Into the Wisdom of Friends and Colleagues

So I turned to one of my other favorite ways to learn and figure things out. I knew that some people seem to be naturally and consistently on time. This has always been intriguing to me. How could they be on time with seemingly little or no effort when I struggle with it, and often end up late anyway? I wanted to find out if they used some strategies or had a way of thinking about their appointments that helped them to be on time. My hope was that I could learn from them and apply the methods successfully in my own life.

I had had success with other learning projects by asking friends and colleagues for their ideas and advice and suggestions. I hoped that I could find similar success by asking for help with the challenge of how to be on time and how to avoid being late. I call this approach "Social Learning" because it is learning from the experience and perspective of the people around me.

I asked many of my friends and colleagues about their methods for being on time and not late for appointments and events. If they were willing to write about their ideas, I asked them to share their advice and experience by writing a chapter for this book. I asked them to do this in an encouraging, positive, uplifting tone, not in a lecturing or condemning way. Most of us who have trouble with being on time have had far too many of those negative messages! We are hungry for something helpful and for a feeling of hope that we really can learn to be on time.

After I heard their ideas and techniques, I spent the next several months experimenting with the strategies they shared with me. I wanted to see which of their ideas might work for me. I wanted to see if I really could be on time more often. Some of the methods I tried were about the timing and sequencing of my actions as I get ready to leave for appointments. Other changes were more subtle and involved shifting my mindset and where I focus my attention as I prepare for events and appointments.

Success at Last!

I am very happy to report that I have been experiencing a lot of success as a result of the ideas in this book! I am on time much more often. And even when I am occasionally late, I arrive much closer to the designated time. People around me are starting to notice that I am on time more often too. That is exciting!

I deeply appreciate the wisdom that each of the contributing authors have shared. Through their generous sharing of experience and ideas, I finally have specific methods and techniques that really do work to help me be on time. I would love for you to experience success with being more on time too.

You'll find great tips and techniques in every chapter, and words of encouragement too. As you read each chapter, look for one or two ideas that you can try yourself. Approach it like an experiment. Try it out. Notice how well it works for you.

I found that I had to try some of the tips and techniques several times until I got better at using them. For example, setting my alarm to get up earlier in the morning required several tries to find how much earlier I needed to set my alarm.

Some techniques work differently in different circumstances. For example, when I am travelling away from home, I found that I need at least 15 extra minutes to get ready in the morning compared to when I am at home because my clothes and toiletries are in different places, and it may take extra time for the hotel elevators or for walking if my room is far from the meeting location. This extra time is especially needed if I am travelling with my husband or sharing a room with someone at a conference.

This Book is For You, Or For Someone You Love

As I have talked with other people about this book, there are two responses I often hear. There are people who have challenges being on time themselves. They usually say something like, "I need that book! I'm always late!" The other response I often hear is from a friend or a spouse who says, "I know someone who really needs that book!"

That is why I published this book. I want you to have access to the great ideas and techniques from this wonderful group of authors. I want you to have the opportunity to try them out in your own life. I would love for you to experience success in your quest to be on time!

I invite you to dive in and explore the ideas that each author shares. Each of their chapters is quick and easy to read. You will find practical ideas and words of encouragement. Look for the methods and techniques that will fit your life and your personality. Experiment with them to see which ones will work best for you. I wish you great success on your journey to being on time!

Chapter 1
Oh No, I'm Late Again!
by Kit Rosato

It's funny how things out of your past can set patterns of behavior that can carry over into your future and impact your life for a long time. Let me share a short story with you.

When I was a teenager I loved to sleep in on Saturdays after a week of getting up early for school. Most teenagers need the extra sleep at this stage of life, and if you have teenagers of your own or remember being one yourself, you know what I am talking about. Now, my wonderful mom has always been an early riser, and she use to wake me up early on Saturdays to go shopping with her. I was resistant, wanting to sleep in. With bribes to buy me something new and continual prodding I would finally get up to accompany her. I couldn't sleep anyway with the constant nudging. Thus a pattern was set in my life of hating to get up and moving along if someone else wanted to set time limitations and expectations on me. I didn't want to get anywhere early, heaven forbid, and so I had set up a pattern of resistance that would be with me a long time. My tendency was to procrastinate to the last minute and then rush around getting ready, checking my watch, and leaving in a flurry only to discover on occasion I had left something I needed behind. Envision whirling dervish.

Eventually I matured enough to realize I was creating this time management problem in my life and needed to take personal responsibility for the choices I was making. That's the first secret to learning to be on time. Own the problem and choose to change the behavior. There is no such thing as finding the time to get things done or not be late. Instead you choose the time, schedule it, and get prepared ahead of time, using simple strategies to help you accomplish your goal. You have the same 24 hours as everybody else, and if others can manage their time so can you. And that is the second secret, believing you can do this before you actually do it. It always feels uncomfortable changing a habit, so expect that feeling and just move forward. When you realize that tardiness in your work and personal life is stealing time from others – actually devaluing their time as if you were more important – you will be motivated to change and live with more integrity.

Once you own the problem, believe you can correct it, and desire and choose to be someone who respects other people's time, you are well on your way to never being late again. Here are a few practical tips that have helped me change my behavior. All of these I do the night before so I am prepared in the morning.

1. Create a written list of exactly where I need to go, the time I need to be there, how long it will take to get there, and when I need to leave to accomplish this. I take into account rush hour traffic and always leave a cushion of at least 15 minutes on top of that. Now I use the GPS in my car for directions but before that I would use Mapquest to get the directions if I wasn't

sure how to best reach my destination. The key is to plan for delays so you won't be late.

2. Never again would I jump in my car and find the gas tank empty. Don't you hate that?! I always check to be sure the gas tank is full or I have plenty to at least get me to my destination with a safe margin of error. After my appointment I can always fill up later in the day if necessary.

3. There is a designated spot in my home where I leave my purse or wallet, car keys, cell phone and anything else I will need. I also usually have a post- it note to remind me to grab a bottle of water out of the refrigerator before I go. I never leave home without it! You never know when you might get stuck somewhere and I don't want to be thirsty. It goes without saying to use the facilities too before heading out the door. The last time I was stuck on the freeway without a way to exit due to an accident was pretty uncomfortable. Unforeseen things can happen on occasion and you will be thankful you blocked out some extra time to get to your appointments early.

4. Having something to read with me always makes the waiting more pleasant since my aim is to be early. I love my Kindle or I bring a book with me or a newspaper. The cell phone is great too, to catch up with emails and social media but if you are headed to the doctor's office they usually prefer your cell phones to be off. Set your reading material next to your purse or wallet.

5. Plan what you are going to wear the night before and be sure it fits, is clean, and easily accessible. The same goes for shoes. I have wasted many a precious moment digging through my many boxes of shoes looking for exactly what I want. For men this rarely is an issue.

6. And last but not least set your alarm so you get up on time if your appointment is early! Schedule enough time to shower, get breakfast and coffee, feed your pets, or whatever else you need so you leave the house relaxed and confident you will be on time. If you have to have a Starbucks coffee schedule enough time for that stop too. Sometimes it is the little extras that put a smile on your face and lift your spirits about an early appointment.

The above tips are really just about organizing your time and space to meet your obligations in a timely manner and feel great about yourself. You can change your old habit of tardiness and procrastination if you really want to. And if something unexpected does delay you in spite of all your planning be sure to call and let others know you will be late or to reschedule. Respecting others time and your own will put you well on to the path of being a person who can be counted on where you rarely have to say "Oh no, I am late again!"

Kit Rosato is a mom of two awesome adult kids (who she usually lets sleep late on Saturdays), happy wife to an incredible guy, and an online entrepreneur who loves marketing, books, and selling on Amazon. She is passionate about learning, growing her business, and helping and inspiring others to do the same. Please stop by her site to say hello and connect with her further at http://KitRosato.com.

Chapter 2
Punctual Meets Tardy: Making a Well-Synchronized Relationship

by Steve Arensberg

I once told my wife that if she were one of the seven dwarfs her dwarf name would be "Tardy." I imagined a cross between Doc and the white hare from Alice in Wonderland, with the waistcoat and the big pocket watch. I thought it was funny. She didn't see the humor...

My wife is perpetually late. "On time" for her is fifteen to twenty minutes after the scheduled time, sometimes half an hour. She does try to be on time, and I try to help her be on time, but all things being equal, she will be late.

I, on the other hand, was educated in the School of Early. I'm not as chronically early as my mother—who will arrive at least fifteen, if not thirty, minutes before her scheduled arrival time—but I would prefer to arrive at least five or ten minutes early. The more important the event (concert, play, interview, etc.) the earlier I like to be.

For me, being on time is a sign of respect for the other person, of showing respect for them and their time. Even when I know the other person will be late (as often happens waiting for the doctor half an hour or more past the scheduled time), I still want to be on time.

When I know I'm going to be late for something, I stress. This adds another layer of angst to whatever event we're planning to attend, or adds stress to what would otherwise be a fun and enjoyable outing.

All of this is less important for my wife. For her, if she's within that fifteen or so minutes after the start of the appointment, that's good enough. She expects that she'll be at least a little bit late, so she's not stressed like I am when she sees the clock ticking away and we haven't left the house yet.

So, as a couple, we found ourselves regularly at odds over those twenty minutes, between my five minutes early and her fifteen minutes late.

If you're anything like us, you're probably struggling with many of the same things we did. And, if you're like us, you learned that the most important thing to do when faced with something like this (or any other point of discord or disagreement) is to talk about it.

As we talked about our situation, it became clear that some of what was occurring was just misunderstanding. When my wife would say "It's not a big deal" when we were going to be late for something, I took that as a dismissal of my feelings, as her not hearing that being on time is important to me. That timeliness is a sign of respect, and it's important to me to be respectful. Once she understood these things about me, she was able to put my stress in perspective, and help me constructively deal with it when we are going to be late.

I, in turn, have learned that my wife's situation is less about being late, and more about her having difficulty estimating time—what I refer to as "time sense." As we talked, I discovered that where I can tell how much time has passed with a fair degree of accuracy (five minutes or so), she has a very difficult time judging how much time something has taken. This also makes it difficult for her to estimate how much time it will take to do something.

I also found out that this is something that really frustrates her about herself. She would like to be more time sensitive, but her brain just doesn't work that way. And my getting stressed out about time often makes her feel more frustrated, and soon we're in a negative pattern.

Does any of this sound like you and your spouse? If it does, you might try some of the strategies below.

Timeliness Strategies

We've experimented with a number of strategies over the years to help us be more on time, to be graceful to ourselves and others when we are late, and to be less uptight about time in general.

Very often, our trouble began with the first appointment of the day. We faced not only the struggles of waking with the alarm clock (never fun), but also of all the morning routine activities, like showering, choosing clothes, doing hair and makeup, and so on.

As I mentioned above, it's difficult for my wife to judge the amount of time it will take to do these things. In her defense, women do seem to have more things to do, and more decisions to make, than men do when getting ready. The difficulty is not in the amount of time itself, as much as it is in judging accurately the amount of time it will take to accomplish these tasks, and get us out the door to arrive where and when we're scheduled.

To combat the problem of the first appointment of the day (and the domino effect that often follows) we've devised several strategies that help us stay on time:

1. **We schedule important appointments later in the day.** When at all possible, we schedule important, time-sensitive meetings later in the day. This allows us to get all the morning rituals done with plenty of time to spare.

2. **We schedule something not time-sensitive before a more time-sensitive appointment.** If we're going to the theater, we might arrange for dinner first, so we have time to get downtown, park, and eat a nice meal all in plenty of time to be comfortably in our seats for an 8 o'clock curtain. Similarly, we might meet for lunch or coffee before an early-afternoon appointment.

3. **I help her prep the night before.** If we are meeting someplace in the morning, or she's headed to work, she and I work through choices of clothes, jewelry, and hairstyle the night before. This allows us plenty of time to try out different options, and to decide on the best one the night before. Then in the morning the decisions are all made, and she can just execute. We find this cuts her morning preparation time at least in half.

We also have learned some other strategies that we apply no matter when the appointment is:

1. **I set the clocks in our vehicles ahead a bit.** I don't tell her how much, but usually it's 7-8 minutes. I don't quite know why this works, but we seem to get closer to being on time when the clocks are fast. A Jedi mind-trick, perhaps? We just know that it seems to shave at

least a few minutes off our time when we do this, so we stick with it!

2. **I tell her an earlier start time.** For example, if the show at the theater is at 8pm, I tell her it starts at 7pm. This is more important when the whole family is doing something, and our two teenagers (also time-sense-challenged) need to be ready to go as well.

3. **I pick her up when we need to go somewhere together,** rather than meeting her at the appointment. This allows me to control the time we leave the house or her office, so that I can make sure she doesn't get caught up in doing "just one more task."

4. **I use non-time-specific words when talking to her about leaving for an appointment.** Since my wife can't process "We have to leave in 15 minutes," I say things like "What do you have left to do? What can I help with?" This way, she's not struggling to figure out how much time she needs and whether that matches the time we have left. I do the time sense work, and suggest which things need to get done now, which can be done on the way, and which just need to be let go.

5. **She stays calm when she sees that I'm stressing.** Her signal to me is to put a hand on my shoulder, and ask "What can I do to help?" I'll suggest something, or just say "Thanks for asking." Mostly this is her acknowledging that she understands this is important to me, and she's working with me to do our best to get there.

6. **If we are going to be late, the navigator calls the place to let them know.** This is our rule for being late: when I know we're going to be late, I'll let her know, and then whoever is not driving will call ahead to let them know we're late and how long we will be. More than any one thing, this simple act does a lot for me to help decompress when I'm stressing. I may still stress about being late in the first place, but doing the

considerate, respectful thing of calling ahead takes a big weight off.

Applying these strategies has made a big difference for us. Not only are we more often on time for our appointments and meetings and events, but we also both arrive in a much improved frame of mind—more relaxed, less irritable, more attuned to each other.

What better way to get the most out of each appointment or event or gathering—or any other activity on which we've chosen to spend our precious time?

Steve Arensberg writes at the intersection of story, inspiration, and self-improvement. His blog, http://freeofgravity.com , offers aspiring heroes help revealing their origin stories and increasing self-knowledge, defining their purpose, and creating habits and practices to build their heroic self.

Chapter 3
What Time Does the 10 a.m. Meeting Start?

by Nita Bauer

With so much technology available to keep track of our appointments and remind us to be on time, it's surprising that so many people are still late for their appointments. I can't tell you how many times my co-workers and I have asked, "What time does the 10 a.m. meeting start?" while waiting for someone to show up. Personally, I wouldn't characterize myself as someone who is on time 100% of the time, either. I'm probably in the 60/40 range. What I've noticed is that my rate of decline depends on the degree of focus I put on these four key elements: impact, intention, commitment, and technology.

Being Aware of the Impact

By far the most important element that motivates me to be on time is the impact on me if I'm late. That could be anything from missing my flight or having an important appointment cancelled, to coming face-to-face with my boss, or just flat embarrassment at being the last one to walk into the room. Of course, if there is no impact on me, my timeliness is more likely to slip. And if there is a persistent impact on me for being on time, like when the party I'm meeting is late, my timeliness will slip even more.

Sure, when I'm only thinking about myself, it's easy to see the impact when other people are late. Years ago, my former husband left me waiting thirty-minutes in a monsoon because he forgot to pick me up from class. Now, I have an almost physical reaction when the person I'm meeting leaves me waiting, monsoon-season or otherwise. But it's equally important to me to avoid causing that same reaction for the people in my life, if I can help it. Of course, not everyone responds with the same fury, but if you think about it, there is almost always an impact when you're late, be it in how the people you're meeting are left feeling about the situation, the success of the meeting, or the potential delay to the schedule. When I choose to be responsible for the impact my timeliness has on myself and others, I can almost always be on time.

Being Intentional About It

I've noticed, though, that being responsible for the impact on myself and others isn't always enough to get me where I'm going in a timely manner. Sometimes I have to build in a little intentionality. In the past few years, I've been taking evening courses in Austin—an hour's drive from my home that easily becomes two hours in rush hour traffic. To get there on time, I have to pre-plan my trip, carry a meal to eat on the road, leave work early, and stay focused on the drive—being ever vigilant for the best lane to drive in to keep my progress from being bogged down by less intentional drivers. The greater the distance to my intended destination, the more intentional I have to be to compensate for unexpected delays in route. Getting there early affords me the added benefit of being able to relax and freshen up before the evening starts, while being late leaves me feeling rushed and unsettled through the whole evening. I'm sure if I put that much intentionality in the rest of my meeting schedule, I could bump up my on-time rate by more than 10%.

Being Committed to Being on Time

Sometimes all the responsibility and intentionality in the world isn't enough to get me where I need to be on time, especially if I have a negative connotation associated with the event, or I just don't want to be there. Going to the dentist, traffic court, or a sit-down with the boss have a way of driving up the child in me, and my resistance to "visiting the principal" syndrome shows up in being late, even when there is a negative impact. I set the snooze button one too many times, let myself get involved in a project or conversation to distract myself, or wait until the last minute to find out exactly where I need to be or how to get there. I'm late, and "it's not my fault the phone rang as I was walking out the door."

On the other hand, if it is something I want to do, something I'm excited about, or something I'm committed to, there is a message center in my brain that lights up with "don't forget; today's the xyz event." I find myself looking at the clock periodically throughout the day. I do the prep work at the same time I schedule myself for the event. I want this, and I will be there—on time! I don't care if the phone is ringing.

If I want to up my game, I have to shift the context for myself, and find a way to be committed to showing up on time even when it is something I dread. Sometimes it's as simple as being committed to fulfilling on doing what I said I would do, or representing myself in a way I want to be remembered—like being someone who is consistent, dependable and reliable. If nothing else, I know my timeliness is communicating the degree of honor and respect I have for other people, and in the end that has a major impact on how they perceive me. You're right; my being on time is all about the impact on me.

Implementing a Technology System that Works

Knowing what drives me is the key to finding the right strategy. If I want to be someone who shows up on time, I can make a point of relating to the impact my being late has on myself and others. I can be intentional about it, plan ahead, stay focused on the act of getting there on time. And I can generate a level of commitment—even for a 10:00 am meeting that will probably start late, go over, and accomplish nothing. All that's left is to find the right technology to keep my brain from flipping the snooze button on me.

A. **Tried and True.** I love any technology that gives me a reminder. My email system has a calendar that gives me pop-up reminders at a predesignated time before the meeting starts. It syncs with my smart phone and that gives me reminders, too. How cool is that? Of course, the default reminder 15 minutes before the meeting is too soon for some meetings, and too late for others. Here's what I do:

a. *Everything* I plan to do at a scheduled time goes in my electronic calendar. All the information I need about where, when, what to bring, and who to contact is added to the meeting notes. Sometimes I put a map of the location for future reference, or copy in my confirmation numbers for flights and hotels.

b. I include the date and actual time of the event in the summary line of the meeting.

c. I set the actual date, but I set the start time for when I need to leave to get there on time and the end time for when I available to be scheduled for something else.

d. I set the reminder for 2 weeks out for anything more than a month away, and 1 or 2 days out for anything I need to do this week that I know I might forget. Then I snooze at reasonable intervals so I get reminded enough times that it syncs with my brain.

e. Events that have prep-work include an additional appointment at some prior date to remind me to accomplish the task.

f. Saturday, Sunday and Monday morning events always get a Friday reminder.

g. If I need 5 minutes to get there on time, I snooze my 15 minute reminder until 5 minutes before, or use that time to collect my things and visit the restroom. If I can, I avoid answering the phone or starting a quick email. They are never quick.

B. **Trick your Brain.** Of course when my brain gets used
    to the way I do things, all the reminders fade into the
    background. I don't hear the little ding anymore, and I
    clear the reminders without reading them. That's
    when it's time to do something else.

   h. Sometimes I color-code my appointments so
       they show up on my calendar in a way that my
       brain is attracted to. Yellow, orange and red
       really catch my eye.
   i. I have a paper calendar on my desk, and I clip
       business cards and notes to it. I write in bold
       colors, big letters, words my brain will be
       attracted to. Sometimes I highlight, underline
       or circle with a different color.
   j. Sticky notes, heck yeah. Bathroom mirror, car
       mirror, coffee pot, refrigerator, front door; I've
       even attached them to the face of my cell
       phone. Whatever technology works!
   k. Of course, you have to look at your reminders.
       It's bad when you have to leave notes to
       remind yourself to read your notes, and stick
       to remember to look at your calendar.

C. **Other Resources**. I like to engage the people in my
    life to help me be on time, too. My daughter loved
    being the "reminder lady" when she was young. Of
    course a license to nag goes a long way, so be careful
    who you invite to take on this role. And, as a
    safeguard, whenever I'm meeting someone at an
    offsite location, I typically ask them to call me ahead of
    time to confirm. In addition to helping me remember
    the event, this has the added benefit of making sure
    I'm not standing in the rain, waiting for my ride to
    show up. Grrr!

Things Happen

Sure. You put your heart and soul into being on time. You even attach a buzzer to your chair to get you up at the precise moment you need to go. But things do fall out of the sky and land on your perfectly planned schedule. It is inevitable that at least some of the time you will be late. That's the perfect time to look at what you can put in place for next time. You can't avoid everything, but with a little commitment and intentionality you can avoid the nasty impact on yourself and others by finding the next technology solution to get you where you're going in a timely manner – Hey what if I record the barking dog and set that to play on my phone instead of the ding?

Nita Bauer is a talented author who writes fiction for young people. As of this writing her first novel is nearing publication. You can learn more at http://NitaBauer.com.

Chapter 4
My Challenge To Be On Time
by Cheryl A. Major

My father would be amazed, or perhaps delighted, that I had been given the opportunity to contribute to a book about being on time. I drove him pretty much nuts with my consistent ability and dedication to being late from early childhood on. So much so, that I remember my family waiting for me in what was probably the 1950 dark green Buick with the dark green visor over the front windshield; my father in the driver's seat, singing, "and here comes the old cow's tail" as I finally emerged from the back door to join the waiting gang in the car. My dad grew up on a dairy farm in Nova Scotia, so I'm sure this had some special significance to which I was not privy; I knew enough to be aware it was not a compliment on my inability to be on time.

The thing that always amazed and baffled me was that no one else in my family had challenges with being on time. I had two sisters who were always on time, and for my parents, punctuality was not an issue. I eventually realized that there was about a 15 minute margin of error, so that no matter what I seem to try, I would be about 15 minutes late for everything. To this day, I truly don't understand why everyone gets so wound up about being right on the dot for an appointment. In spite of my point of view however, it seems to be a big deal to most people, so I've spent a good bit of time honing my punctuality skills and trying different methods of dealing with my "inner clock" that just runs 15 minutes late.

In grade school, I would often miss the school bus. The big yellow bus with a number 5 on it circled around and came back just as a normal route about 10 minutes after the initial stop, which I routinely would miss, so I was lucky the bus driver would stop and pick me up on his way back. Other times, I would miss both opportunities, so walking or riding my bike to school would get me there.

Writing this is a good exercise because I am reminded that I once noticed one of my sisters figuring out in her head how long the different tasks would take that she had to complete to get herself ready and out the door on time. I never broke my getting ready stuff into bits like that. Hmmm.....maybe that's the next method I'll develop and try on myself...

I annoyed such a sufficient number of friends and family members with my tardiness that it became necessary to address my bad habit. From blatant, unabashed and wanton lateness, I eventually moved on to setting my clocks and my watch ahead so I would have some buffer...some time to spare. Actually no time to spare; I just wouldn't be quite so late. In addition, I knew when I looked at the clock or at my watch that I still had more time, so this was not really the answer.

My husband, who is never late, was always annoyed that I would be home 15 to 30 minutes later than what I predicted my ETA would be. This was the subject of "animated discussion" on more than one occasion.

One day, a few years ago, I remember getting my car back from having some repairs made. I had to reset the clock in my car. I went to set it 5 minutes ahead; my recent customary habit. I stopped and said to myself, "This is ridiculous...it's not making me be on time..." That moment was the beginning of a change in my habits. The car clock, the clock in the bedroom and my watch all started running on real time. I began to prepare differently to get out the door. I started getting up earlier as I really need a little "me" time in the morning just to do some reading and/or writing before I get to the rest of my day. I found I had more energy when I got up earlier too. That was a surprise for someone who always considered herself a night owl!

Living on real time and just dealing with it has made a big difference. One of the things I do now is before I go to bed, I look at my schedule (which is always different), and I figure out when I have to leave the house. I write down what time I need to leave on a piece of paper that I leave on the kitchen counter so I can't miss it when I get up. That reminds me what my time frame that morning is, and it helps keep me on task. To be honest, I build in a little "Cheryl runs late" time into that departure time. I can't claim to be comfortably out the door; I still seem to rush at the last minute, but I'm working on that.

I also use the alarm on my smart phone. This allows me to focus on what I'm doing during the day instead of having to keep an eye on the time and worrying about when I need to leave for an appointment or an important meeting. I usually set the alarm for 15 minutes before I need to be out the door so I can wrap up what I'm doing, and you remember my 15 minute late inner clock story...

I began to notice that I like being on time. I like not making excuses. This surprised me, but it certainly reinforced my efforts to reform my views on punctuality. Occasionally I still run late, but if it's just my fault, I own up to it rather than blame traffic or the slow poke in front of me on a single lane road. By the way, why is it that when you're in a hurry, someone always seems to peel out in front of you at the last minute and then drive for the next few miles at 20 miles an hour!? Is it just me??

There you have it; I'm not totally recovered, but a work in progress. I do much better these days though, and it's a much more comfortable habit to adopt.

I've noticed that recently my biggest nemesis is that I think I can do "just one more thing" and still make it somewhere on time. That doesn't always end well... And so my punctuality rehab continues...

You can learn more about Cheryl A. Major at http://ThinStrongHealthy.com where she shares as she learns. Join us there; take what you can use now, and come back often to grow with our community as we teach ourselves to eat well, love what we eat, and be happy! Live, love, laugh, and make Major improvements in your life!

Chapter 5
Respecting Time – Yours and That of Everyone Around You

by Connie Ragen Green

I was about fifteen when I realized that my punctuality was an inherited trait. My father, whom I did not see very often while I was growing up, and I had gone to lunch and the topic came up. It turned out that both of us made a concerted effort to never be late to any type of meeting or appointment and disliked it immensely when someone kept us waiting. I saw this as a way to become closer with my father and did not realize just how much it would affect my life as I grew older.

In college my classes at UCLA were so far apart because of the vastness of the campus. Even though I was a commuter I kept a bicycle at school so that I could easily make it to each class before the top of the hour. I would cringe when I saw students coming in five, ten, or even more minutes late, knowing they had missed crucial information that would hurt them over the course of the quarter.

My first job after graduating from college was with a commercial bank. They emphasized the need to be on time for work each morning and for breaks and lunch periods. When you think of 'banking hours' you don't give any leeway for tardiness or exceptions to the rule. When I was subsequently robbed at gunpoint twice during my time there I believe it was much easier for them because of the precise schedule we kept in regards to moving and storing the cash within our walls.

At age thirty I became a classroom teacher, and each day consisted of a bell schedule that had to be strictly adhered to at all times. These bells began at seven fifteen in the morning and denoted the opening of the front gate, the time to line up, when to go into the classroom, the first recess, lunch, and dismissal. In addition, there were bells for designated activities throughout the day such as a special event to be held on the yard, the 'rainy day' schedule announcement, and so many more. I became so accustomed to this bell schedule that I would actually salivate thirty seconds prior to the recess bell, knowing that my snack awaited me.

Not everyone valued and embraced punctuality at the school. The students who continued to be habitually late usually got their act together during the first month of school because they did not want to suffer the consequences, such as being excluded from activities and receiving the disapproving looks from their peers.

There were several teachers for whom this was also an issue, but they did not change their ways while I knew them. Instead, the other teachers were forced into picking up the slack on a daily basis. It was not unusual for me to have two or three classrooms of students (more than a hundred kids) following my line back into class after recess or lunch because their own teacher was nowhere to be found. The principal was more than a little perturbed by this, but our union prevented the administrators from taking any action. This caused a great divide among all of us, with the tardy teachers feeling like they had pulled a fast one on the system and the punctual ones feeling overburdened and resentful. When it was time for me to do a project with a group of teachers, or to arrange a field trip, I always looked for those who I knew would respect time as much as I did.

Why Are People Late?

That's a difficult question to answer, but it is my firm belief that lack of planning and organizational skills are at least partially to blame. You have an obligation to yourself and to others to be well prepared for your day. For me this begins the evening before. I know what I will need the following day and I begin to gather it all together right after dinner.

I also taught this strategy to my students during my twenty years as a classroom teacher. On a regular basis I took them through scenarios of how I was preparing for the following day. It started with a list of what I would need. Everything would go into my school bag, which was then set by my front door. If something could not be placed into the bag that night, such as something that needed to stay refrigerated until the following morning, I would write it on a small notepad that was next to the door. If I was already in bed and thought of something else that I needed, I would get out of bed and put the item into the bag or write it on the note. During those twenty years I can count on one hand the times I forgot to bring something to school with me that I needed.

The next morning was then a relatively easy one. I maintained the same routine of walking my dogs, eating breakfast, showering and dressing, and then leaving for the day. Without the need to scurry around and locate what I needed, I had plenty of time to enjoy my morning.

Fast forward twenty years and I have now started my online business. It takes a few months before I realize that being on time is even more important now. I have self-imposed deadlines on things such as blog posts, podcasts, information products, teleseminars and webinars, and live events. Those who are punctual and reliable enjoy the best opportunity for success. Because many of us have not met in person, one misstep can cost you a relationship and all that goes along with that.

You may have noticed that I added a new word here - reliable. In my thinking, reliability goes hand in hand with honesty, loyalty, and trustworthiness. It's that wonderful quality some people have that means they do what they say they will do, when they said they would do it. They not only do it, but they do it with a sense of true commitment and a positive attitude. They are trustworthy and their word is their bond. No one plays a role in my business life, whether it is a virtual assistant, travel agent, housekeeper, dog groomer, dentist, or other support person who does not understand and practice these qualities every single day.

When I was just starting out online and needed to make a name for myself quickly, these were all traits and qualities I wanted to exude so that people who could help me would have great confidence in doing so. This proved to be an excellent strategy in that so many people put their reputations on the line to help me move forward. If someone asked me to be a guest on their teleseminar or webinar, I was on the line eight to ten minutes before we were to begin. When I attended a live event I was right there when the doors opened to take my seat and be ready for the day.

Now I teach people how to become online entrepreneurs and I see the same type of behavior I witnessed as a classroom teacher. Those who are perpetually late are always playing 'catch up' with those who are punctual.

How Can You Train Yourself To Never Be Late Again?

Forget about setting your clocks five or ten minutes ahead or other games or tricks. Instead, spend time on a weekend or other day off to see how long it really takes you to do specific tasks. For example, I can shower in ten minutes if I don't wash my hair and fifteen minutes if I do. I choose clothes the evening before so no time is spent with that in the morning. By doing this day in and day out I can predict precisely how much time I will need to get out the door. Do this with every area of your life and your punctuality skills will improve immensely.

Remember, respecting time will lift you up in the eyes of everyone you encounter, and boost your confidence as well.

Connie Ragen Green is an online marketing strategist and bestselling author living in southern California. She teaches people on six continents how to build profitable online businesses so they may live the life they choose. Find out more at http://ConnieRagenGreen.com.

Chapter 6
Going Somewhere? Arrive Early or at Least On Time
by Jim Symcox

It's such a simple concept that most of us overlook it.

Think how it could change the world if everyone showed up early or at least on time for work, school, appointments, airports, dates, weddings, child visitations, and family gatherings. I know people who show up late for everything: classes, concerts, church, movies, client appointments, work, lunch, dinner. I honestly don't think they ever think about the people on the other end waiting and wondering where they are, or if something bad has happened to them en route between where they were and their destination.

I don't know if the desire or need to be early or on-time or chronically late is an innate quality or a learned behavior.

Maybe it's some of both. However, what I do know is that there are people in both camps.

My Dad was a Master Sergeant (the highest ranking NCO) in the Army and fought in the Pacific Theatre of World War II. The military has a motto: "if you aren't five minutes early, you're late." Then there's the old saying: "if you're five minutes early, you're on time. If you're on time, you're late. And if you're late, you're fired!" I am sure that his influence on me has something to do with my preference to being early or on time.

I grew up on a farm in the Panhandle of Texas, northwest of Lubbock. My Dad was a fantastic farmer and raised crops of cotton, corn, milo/grain sorghum, and wheat. I spent my entire upbringing learning life experiences and lessons from my Dad on that farm. One of the greatest lessons was how to respect our most precious commodity, time. Time is a finite commodity of life. We are given an exact amount of time, and we don't know the amount of that allotment. Nothing we do can create more of it or prolong what's been allocated. On the farm, in order to survive, one must do things in a very prompt and timely manner. Spring is characterized by planting. It is a time to plant a vegetable garden, or flowers and shrubs, and for farmers, it is a time to plant their crops. Now planting assumes that there will be a time to harvest. So springtime is a very busy time of the year for most folks, and they look forward to the time when they will be able to see the results of their labor. Be late for planting and most likely there isn't going to be a harvest worth having.

As a high school freshman baseball player, I was blessed with God-given talent and physical ability to be on our varsity baseball team. Our coach, Vernon Scott, had a hard and firm rule: Be early or on-time and ready to go when the bus was scheduled to leave for road games or be left behind. This was non-negotiable and no exceptions would be made. I found that out when I was late getting out of class one day in order to make it to the field house early enough to make the bus. I arrived just in time to see the bus pulling out of the parking lot. You can bet your last nickel that never happened to me again.

To me being early or on-time is a matter of respect for others, valuing other people more than yourself, showing others genuine appreciation and also having a healthy self-respect. I have found that people who are habitually late offer very little, if any of that to others. I also believe some people are late because they have a strong sense of entitlement. It's a lack of regard for the needs, rights and expectations of others. They feel they can do things on their own time, and they really don't care that they're late and you've been waiting. Overall, to be chronically late is simply rudeness.

I'll be totally honest with you, I hate waiting for people. Who doesn't? You start to get irritated and wonder if they'll ever show up. I have a 30 minute rule. If you don't show up within 30 minutes of our agreed-upon time, our plans are off and I'm out of there.

What are the downsides to being late? It upsets people when you're late. People see you as rude and disrespectful-- and they are right. People think you're inconsiderate, incompetent, and self-centered-and they're right. You get a bad reputation. People think they can't count on you. If they can't trust you to show up on time, how can they trust you to follow through with other commitments? They don't take you seriously. Your word is no good. Being late causes stress for you and everyone else. It creates a roller coaster ride of emotions. Being late can also be a very expensive proposition. During my years as a Texas State Trooper one of the most common excuses I received for those people I stopped for speeding was they were late to get somewhere. If they had planned better, made being where they were going a higher priority, then fewer speeding tickets would have been issued and just think of the money saved. Everyone has enough time to factor in for detours and delays.

Sure, you can offer apologies and promises you don't intend to keep. You end up telling lies or half truths about why you're late to make yourself look better. You embellish on how bad the traffic was half a block away and you got stuck behind the school bus or how slow the lady was driving in front of you, when the truth is you were late because you overslept, tried to squeeze in one more activity on the way out the door, didn't leave enough room between commitments, or never determined how long it would take you to get to the event.

Being late hurts relationships. Imagine how awful your children feel when you're late for their school and sporting events. It's terrible to make them worry about whether you're going to show up and see them play football, basketball, baseball, soccer, or whether you arrive at the school play or recital to watch them perform their solo.

Then there are the divorced parents who are late to pick up their child for their weekend visitation. The child stands at the window and watches in tears as each car passes and it isn't mom or dad. Why make them fret that you forgot them? Arrive before they're at the window. Put their minds at ease and arrive early so they know you value them and your time together. Don't let them think for a second that you don't care, that you won't show up. Being late is a poor behavior to model for them. Don't teach them to make people wait for them, that it's okay to make a grand entrance and get cheap ego strokes at the expense of others by walking in late.

I've seen people walk in late at funerals and weddings, which draws attention to them instead of the person everyone is gathered to celebrate or honor.

For some people it's a power game, a way to control others by making them wait. You get to hold up the spinning of their world. For others, it's a cheap way to rebel and create some drama.

Some people are chronically late because they can't say no and don't leave enough room for all the things they said yes to. But are you really saying yes to something if you're going to miss it by being late?

You wouldn't consider being late for a job interview. You want to make a great first impression and walk in the door five minutes early. But once you get the job, you show up five minutes late every day and think nothing of it.

There are benefits for being early or on-time. I schedule in breathing room. That gives me time to get a decent parking space, make calls in the parking lot, hit the restroom, relax, pray, pause, prepare, and just breathe.

Below are some of my favorite strategies for being on time.

When I travel by air, I arrive two hours before a flight. In the old days, you could run through the airport, run to the gate, and hop on the flight as the plane was pulling out. Not anymore. I leave extra room in case there's a high-security alert, traffic on the drive, a flat tire, a parking lot situation, or long lines in TSA security check lines or to board. It feels good to check in with room to spare to read a book, check e-mails, eat, de-stress, and prepare for what's on the other end.

Check the weather the night before so you have your coat or umbrella at the door. Choose what you'll wear the night before, pack your lunch, fill the gas tank and wallet with cash for lunch and parking. I keep my keys in the same place every day, in my hat by the door, so I never waste time looking for them.

I believe it's very important to think through what I put on the calendar before the ink hits the paper. I pause before saying yes and ask each person what kind of time commitments this will involve. Then I pause and ask myself what I will be giving up to say yes to this. Everything is a trade-off. Every time you say yes, you're saying no to something or someone else, to include yourself. I have no problem saying no if I have any hint this is going to be a waste of precious time.

When it comes to completing tasks, I give each one an amount of time. You can't manage time, you can however manage tasks. How much time will it really required? That way, each day on the calendar isn't full of a stack of to do's that can't possibly fit into a 24-hour day.

Instead of being predictably late, you could be the one most likely to show up early, the one everyone can count on. Life is unpredictable, but you don't have to be.

Jim Symcox is the President of Hard Facts – Soft Skills. Jim is a highly sought after business consultant, executive leadership coach and speaker. Former Texas state trooper, entrepreneur, and corporate executive, Jim brings a uniquely powerful perspective and incredible resume to improving individual and team performances, productivity, profitability and significant positive results in organizations.

Editor's Note: Sadly, Jim Symcox passed away shortly before publication of this book. He will be deeply missed by all who knew him.

Chapter 7
Being On-Time:
Strategies From The Empty Nest Authority

by Dorine Kramer, M.D.

Being on time has never come naturally to me, but as an Empty Nester the challenge became almost insuperable until I discovered three critical ideas. One of these is a concept I learned from NLP (neurolingistic programming). The second is based in the study and practice of personal integrity. The last is a mindset I actually learned from my daughter.

Before I tell you how I conquered my lateness habit, allow me tell you why it was always so difficult for me to be on time. In my family late was the norm and on time was the exception. I suppose it must have been different for my dad— I'm sure he wasn't late for business appointments or for his recording gigs as a violinist with the CBS network orchestra. But for family events, and certainly for my mother and me, "Jewish standard time" was the norm and the excuse, and that meant half an hour late for just about everything!

As a college student I struggled valiantly against my upbringing to get to school on time, dashing into lecture halls just as the bell sounded the beginning of class. Imagine my dismay when many classes I wanted to take were only offered at 8 am—four days a week! It was not worth the threat to my grade point average to be late, so I devised a system that worked for me then. I scheduled racquetball games even earlier, at 6 am. I didn't want to disappoint my partner or waste court time by being late, and the timing was perfect to get me to class by 8. I managed to get to those 8 am classes for several years with that system, which was my first experience with what I now think of as voluntary accountability.

Later, when I worked at the Centers for Disease Control, I used the flexi-time option to deal with my proclivity for being late. As long as I made up the time at the end of the day, I could come late in the morning. But when I left that position, things had to change.

I married a man who prided himself on appearing for appointments (and dates) on time to the second, literally, and although I still was often late, I started to notice that there are some people in the world who actually value being punctual, i.e., honoring an agreement to be somewhere or meet someone at a particular time.

Still it was a shock some years later when I was informed by a friend that she took it as a personal insult when I was late, because it meant I didn't think her time was as important as mine. It had honestly never occurred to me that I was being selfish, and it created a shift for me and my attitude toward being on time, but it didn't lessen the struggle.

The clincher was when my young daughter, aged about 6, informed me that she was embarrassed when she walked in late, even just a few minutes late, to school or to a lesson. It wasn't OK with me to do that to her, so I had to be on time, whatever it took. And I was on time, much of the time, for many years for selected events and people. But it was never easy or natural.

Fast forward about twenty years. I found myself with an empty nest... and the rules changed. Everything changed. I couldn't use the tools and incentives that had forced me to pay attention to the time and be where I said I would when I said would. Those tools no longer existed. All the routines of school hours, after-school activities, and kids' carpools vanished, and then my husband retired and his schedule and routines vanished. There was no longer a structure which kept me in line without making me truly responsible for being on time. And then I started my own business and had to find a way to take back that responsibility.

What I Learned From NLP

In NLP, there is a concept called a timeline. Mine may look different from yours, but we all have one.

What is a timeline? It's essentially an imaginary line which holds your personal history. You can find yours by standing up, closing your eyes, and answering the questions "If you could see them, where would your past be? Where would your future be? Where is the present moment?" It can be straight or zigzag or spiral. It can go left to right, right to left, front to back, up to down. There is no right or wrong answer.

There are many ways to use your timeline in NLP processes. But the aspect that I found useful and relevant here, and that you may find useful, is that your timeline can help you figure out how you perceive time.

For instance, if you see the whole line in front of you, with your past to your left, your future to your right, and the present directly in front of you, you are probably a "through-time" person and are less likely to have trouble keeping to a schedule.

If your line goes from your past behind you, right through you in the present, and off ahead of you into your future, you are most likely an "in-time" person, and you may get so involved in what's going on in any given moment that you forget about the time—you don't pay much attention to it, and don't really notice when it's time to stop what you are doing and go do something else or be somewhere else.

The terminology isn't important. But the idea that there are some people who just don't comprehend getting lost in the moment and losing track of the time is very helpful. Likewise, knowing that some people don't understand how anyone can possibly be obsessed with being on time provides another perspective. Whichever one you are, it's helpful to know so you understand why you are the way you are about timeliness and you can take steps to manage your own time when you need to.

What Is This Integrity Thing?

My extensive coach training included a specialty training in accountability. Now, I'm sure the word is familiar to you, but I learned a whole new meaning for it in the way we were taught it and the rationale for it. I had to be on time within one minute of the exact appointed time for the group classes and for every coaching call (ten per week with other trainees in Coach University) or I was called out on my lack of accountability.

I wonder if this sounds extreme to you. It seemed so to me initially. But as we went on, I understood.

It is a matter of integrity to keep your agreements. That includes being where you say will be when you say you will be there. If you arrange a call for 10 am and you don't show up at 10 am, you are out of integrity, and there is no room for question.

So I imagine you may be wondering why a minute or two matters. Here's the reason. It is critical to your success in life and business that *you* can believe your own word. Yes, it's more considerate to others, and it's important that they can believe you with certainty. But the thing is, if you know that you can trust yourself to keep your word, then anything you say you will do, you know you will find a way to make happen.

Just imagine what that means for your level of achievement and accomplishment. How about for your self-esteem? How much confidence will you have in yourself and your ability to achieve what you want if you have a history that whatever you say will happen, you will find a way to make it so? If you have consistently been proving your integrity to yourself, this is the situation you will be in.

The Key Mindset that Keeps Me On Time

My most specific and direct technique for staying on time I have to credit to my daughter. Remember the one who hated being late? Well, here's what she taught me: it's all about mindset.

You might be wondering exactly what mindset.

Is it about being considerate and understanding of others who might have a different concept of how important being on time actually is? No!

Is it about staying in integrity? No!

Here it is. Getting to my appointment feeling relaxed, comfortable, and prepared, both physically and mentally, must be more important to me than whatever else I might use those last few minutes for—the minutes that make me rush and possibly be late rather than on time.

It doesn't matter whether it's a telephone appointment or an in-person meeting. I know that if I am rushing to get there, my focus is still on getting there and not on the person or event where I want my focus to be. I am out of breath, metaphorically or even actually, heart racing, anxious, and definitely not at my best. And that is not how I want to feel or to show up. How do you want to show up?

I've talked about some time issues that came up for me specifically when I became an empty nester. But I know it didn't really start there. Perhaps you've had some similar time issues from your upbringing, or perhaps you are an Empty Nester as well. Whatever your own personal situation, keep these ideas in mind. They will help you to be on time, and along the way, you may find you feel better about yourself and about what a great job you are doing with keeping your agreements around time.

Dr. Dorine Kramer is a retired medical doctor, author, speaker, and Empty Nest Authority. She helps empty nest women and women in major life transitions to reinvent themselves, rediscover romance, and re-imagine their futures. You can contact her via her website at
http://www.yourtimetosoar.com
or http://www.drdorinekramer.com

Chapter 8
Success for the
Distractaholic

by Karen Boenig

*"He who would learn to fly one day must first learn to
stand and walk and run and climb and dance; one cannot fly
into flying."*
~Friedrich Nietzsche

Time is one of my biggest challenges in life, and as I age, my struggles are increasing rapidly. When I lived in my parents' home, I was raised to believe that 15 minutes early is on-time, and in my college years, I consistently made it to class on the dot. Tardy tendencies emerged after I got married and began my first career. I was losing my healthy understanding and respect for time, and having children revealed my all-time low. Being chronically late by at least 15 minutes to everything became my new "on-time". This behavior earned me endearing names like "Abby Normal" with my own time zone: KST (Karen Standard Time).

My wonderful, loving parents made it their jobs to support me with prepared hot meals, transportation, and clean laundry. Thanks to their undying devotion to our family, I consistently experienced successful results of a healthy on-time routine. It was beautiful. It was peaceful. It was powerful. It was also taken for granted, and I will be forever grateful to them.

Being chronically late embarrasses my husband and daughters. Being late is disrespectful to family, friends, doctors, teachers, pest control men, and lots more. Being late is ill-mannered and discourteous. It causes others pain, lack of peace, and anger to levels I honestly do not want to know. My late habits have caused me great personal disappointment from missed programs and meetings, wasted opportunities, wrecked cars, acquired speeding tickets, broken, lost or forgotten items, and deeply felt negative emotions.

How could I have fallen so far from the "perfection" I experienced in my youth? Someone must be to blame for my slacking. My husband? My children? No, all fingers point to me.

When left on my own as a responsible adult, I obviously failed the test. Being on time is not genetic and no amount of childhood training automatically equips you with this fine, admirable skill forever and ever. After my wearing the "cone of shame" for decades, a wise, intuitive, and kind doctor told me that no one can expect to be completely organized and on-time when they are consistently pulled in different directions. Do you mean like me? Seriously? That means that I'm not bad? There is a silver lining? My thinking needs adjusting? YES! I can do that. Let the healing begin!

Recently I have been blessed with a temporary gift of time and a chance to get back to basic and fundamental time management skills and attitude. Life is messy and we can let the fast pace and quick changes control us, destroy us, or strengthen us. I've tried the first two. Strength will be a welcome change.

Practicing being on time every day is like the athlete practicing drills or the musician practicing scales. If I ever expect to get stronger, I have to diligently lift and add weights. Therefore, I should practice and celebrate good, respectful, on-time behavior if I expect a smooth rhythm, full of balance and productivity, to most days.

Karen's "Be-On-Time Drills" and tools include:

1. A 16 X 22 inch calendar is essential for me. It is my hub to an entire wall mounted message center. I use the exposed side of my refrigerator, which is not visible to company when entering my home. All doctor appointment cards, children's schedules, dates with friends, football games, and birthday parties get transferred to this calendar. Appointment cards, schedules, and invitations are filed and kept next to this calendar for a quick reference regarding details of the event. The time of every appointment gets written on the calendar 15 to 20 minutes earlier than the actual appointment to allow for KST (Karen Standard Time is 15 minutes late).

2. Electronic tools are so handy, but finding the right one can be a little overwhelming. Smart phones, Microsoft Outlook, Google Calendar, and so on can all assist with keeping us on time. I am searching for the perfect one.

3. Smart phone apps are so fun. My phone screen is paneled with my colorful big picture tiles reminding me several times a day of my well-balanced Decade of Destiny* goals. Being clinically diagnosed with ADHD adds the extra challenge of staying focused for me, so the color tiles, sound, and text app reminders to drink water and get ready for bed may be silly to some, but are as essential to me as the communication buttons.

4. Hand-written checklists are important to me. I respond best to large print written with a Sharpie marker on index cards, and I have grown to love the compact 3 X 5 size and the thickness of card stock. Unlike my well-handled grocery list written on regular 20 pound paper that thoroughly disgusts me when it ends up in several small, sweaty pieces by the time I get to the check-out counter, my index cards on card stock hold up better against the torture I make them endure. Of course, rewriting a new task card after reviewing my calendar and planning my next day is very rewarding. I toss the cards that have become messy with my bold lines drawn with excitement and in celebration of a task that is <u>completely</u> done.

5. Set timers. As I have matured, I realize that big, beautiful chunks of time to accomplish a goal are not always realistic. Breaking up jobs into phases and allowing 7, 15, 30 minutes a day on a project gets the task accomplished more efficiently if I work backwards from the deadline. Planning is imperative for this to happen and the results are actually better than when I plow through in one sitting. Even football teams get four chances to make a first down; I can allow myself more chances than the "one and done" mentality I generally practice by default. Making the most of time snippets or sound bytes has become an incredibly interesting phenomena to me, about which I want to learn more.

Like "that one small, extra Yopp " from the shirker, Jo-Jo, in Dr. Seuss' book <u>Horton Hears a Who</u> helped the tiny town of Whoville be heard from the clover, I received some wisdom that broke through my noise and busyness cloud. I realized an attitude adjustment and careful planning that I don't always feel I have time for will need to happen to cause me to start being on time again. I'm ready to roll up my sleeves and pull out some thought "weeds" at the roots.

I started work on my thought life and breaking some deeply embedded distorted thinking patterns. No, I am not bad and shameful for being late, nor have I permanently hindered my children from any hope of knowing success regarding being on time.

I began setting Decade of Destiny* goals according to a well-balanced life design introduced to me by Rick Warren, Senior Pastor of Saddleback Church in California. The areas are spiritual, physical, financial, emotional-mental, emotional-recreational, relational-family, relational-social, and occupational.

Using The Four Disciplines of Execution by Sean Covey, I learned that lag measures, lead measures, and compelling scoreboards are essential elements for reaching your goals. So I created measurements for reaching the goals of each of the eight areas of life and invited my family to listen, agree, and fully support these new efforts of moving forward into happy and productive lives that are consistently on time and meeting deadlines.

Having the right relationship with time and being on time are very important. Rely only sparingly on the good graces of others. Life was meant to be experienced and lived to the fullest - full of love, full of laughter, and full of learning. Stopping to smell the roses is equally important. With proper planning and the support of others, you can have the best of both worlds.

So boldly replace distorted thinking with truths. Live, love, forgive, and know yourself. Play to your strengths. Lay a firm foundation of balance. Set goals to achieve at least 10 years of balanced living. Create measurements of the goals on a scoreboard that is always highly visible. Now bring out the timekeepers, deadlines and timers to practice on-time skills for a productive and fruitful life every day. There is a whole long abundant life worth getting excited about and celebrating.

I want to leave a lasting legacy of innovation and influence as well as bring value to the marketplace. I know with powerful confidence that no matter what daily curves are thrown my way, I can regroup and get back on course with energy, excitement and celebration because I have confidence in the foundation I have laid and know in advance what direction I am headed. The people I meet, the relationships I build, the things I learn are rich with blessings beyond anything I can plan for in my finite mind. I appreciate it all and never want to miss anything again because I was late.

Karen Boenig is an expert at developing creative marketing strategies for small businesses. She lives in San Antonio with her husband and three beautiful daughters.

Chapter 9
Curtain Goes Up At Eight
by Geoff Hoff

I grew up in the theatre. Okay, not literally, though almost. From my grade school days in a small town in Northern New Jersey where I was in an "assembly" at least once a year, to junior high and high school in Spokane, Washington, where I was in the dreaded drama club. While in high school, I started working at the local civic theatre and dove in full force, acting in plays, performing base fiddle in the orchestras of musicals, working backstage and even directing. And when I finally entered college, my major, no surprise to anyone, was theatre. Notice that I spell that when an "re". Yes, I'm that pretentious.

In any case, I learned early on that when you said, "curtain at 8", that meant that the play started at exactly eight pm sharp, no excuses, no argument. It was so ingrained in me that I didn't even really think about it. When performing, I'd get to the theatre at least a couple of hours early to get ready, mentally and physically, for the show. Getting in to costume and makeup didn't take that long, but I wanted to make sure nothing got in the way of my getting there.

When I got to Los Angeles and started seeing (and being in) plays in the many small theatres that dot the landscape, I was shocked to find that "curtain at 8" often meant that the show started at 8:05, 8:10, even as late as 8:20. The curtain was often "held" because a drama critic from one of the newspapers hadn't shown up, yet (I find that practice abhorrent - both for the critic and the theatre), but more often it was because one of the actors had gotten stuck in traffic, or some such nonsense.

I directed a play and one night during the first week of rehearsals, two of the actors arrived late. I stopped everything and told them in no uncertain terms that it would not happen again. Because I'm generally a very nice guy with a pleasant demeanor, the rare times when I get angry, it can be very effective. No one was ever late to a rehearsal or performance again for the entire run of the play.

In your own life, however, you can't count on having a teddy bear of a director suddenly turn grizzly about tardiness for your inspiration to be on time.

There are several possible reasons why some people are habitually late. Here are a few:

1. You try to get as much done before you leave as you can, and it always takes more time than you'd planned on
2. Lack of planning at all
3. You think your time is more important than other people's time
4. The appointment isn't important enough to you
5. Lack of respect for the people your appointment is with

6. You don't want to be made to wait, so you plan on getting there at the very last moment and that usually ends up being AFTER the very last moment

Some of those may seem a harsh evaluation, but if you are one who is habitually late and you look honestly, at least a couple of these describe you. The first two in the above list can be solved with some planning ahead. You know when your appointment is (and if you don't, get a calendar – either an electronic one or a wall calendar. And use it!)

One of the things I've learned living in LA is that no one allows themselves enough travel time. When planning on getting to your appointment, if travel is involved, schedule in the appropriate amount of time it would normally take to get there. Then double it. That way, if you end up leaving a moment or two late (and if you do that often, you know you will again) you still have some time to spare. It also negates any "I got stuck in traffic" excuses. I call that "Getting Lost Time" but it's not only for going to places you've never been.

When you know you have an appointment, in the hours before, don't plan on starting a project that you know will either take all your concentration to the point that the world will go away or a project that will take hours to set up and start. Either will almost guarantee that you get a late start and end up either being harried, late or both.

The other issues in the list above are a little more problematic. They involve attitude and mind-set, either of which can seem daunting to impossible to attack or attend to. But take heart, they can be dealt with!

The first step (like in that list of 12 things we often hear about) is acknowledging the issue is one you have. If you do tend to feel your time is more important than anyone else's, that your appointments aren't really very important or that you don't respect others' time, start by saying, yeah, that is me.

Now, I imagine you think I'm going to suggest you "slay that dragon!" Quite the opposite. Dragons have a habit of not staying dead. These attitudes are insistent little beasts. Acknowledging them will defuse much of their power. Then, you might be tempted to want to see where they've come from. Just know that most of our dragons are there because at one time they were protecting us from something. Who knows what at this point. Perhaps the hurt received from a misguided friend or an uncomprehending adult. Perhaps the slight from a bully. It's not important to know what, exactly. What is important is to see they are only there for your good. Then you can look at them in a completely different way.

Rather than trying to slay them, consider looking after them, caring for them. Hugging them and softly letting them know how well they've been serving you. Then letting them know you're grateful and that you don't need that protection any more. Then pat them on the fanny and send them outside to play.

Once you do that, your resistance to them will disappear and, as we have been told, that which we resist persists. Once your resistance to them is gone, their power over you will be gone also. Be clear, the dragon, the attitudes and mind-sets, will still be there. They will still creep in when you least want to see them. They were forged in childhood and children need constant reassurance. When they do show up again, repeat the process.

It's a good idea to even plan on your thoughts and attitudes showing up when an appointment is nearing. That's when a little preemptive chat with them may be in order.

In order to be on time habitually and consistently, know your habits. Know your attitudes and the thoughts that you usually have beforehand. Then plan, with those in mind, and give yourself enough time to get to your appointment. Double that, and get there before the curtain goes up.

Geoff Hoff has been a best-selling author of both fiction, how-to and business books. He has also been an actor, an acting teacher, a standup comic and a popular blogger. He teaches creative writing, tech and marketing courses on the Internet. After studying the process of creativity for years, he was amazed to discover that creativity could be practical, it could be taught and it was not only important, but necessary for every entrepreneur. His classes also tend to be a lot of fun. You can find out more about Geoff at http://GeoffHoff.com

Chapter 10
Set Yourself Up For Success:
A Real Life Time
Management Technique
That Works

by Marian LaSalle

Do you ever find yourself in trouble with the people in this world that you care about? In trouble because you're constantly late to appointments? Do you find yourself...

Late to work?

Late to pick up your children from school?

Late for appointments that mean a lot to you?

Well if you said yes, you're not alone. This was my life starting from as long back as I can remember. I recall my teachers being always on my case and even being sent down to the principal's office and punished for being constantly late to school. As I grew a little older I remember being in trouble all the time with my parents for being late. Once I grew old enough to get a job, I was always in trouble with my boss for being late to work and then my spouse for procrastinating so often and making him late.

Most people believe that being late is a choice. If it's always someone else's fault or your excuse list is as long as a child's Christmas list, case closed. Being chronically late also sends a strong message that you believe your time is more valuable than those waiting for you and they have every right to be annoyed. It starts off innocently enough and then it can turn into a BAD habit. If you're honest with yourself and can write down what you think is causing it, you might be able to figure it out. Even if you don't know what's causing it, I have a FABULOUS way to set yourself up to always either be early or at least on-time.

One day I remember thinking to myself I HATE being late all the time, why can't I ever get to my appointments on time? My dearest friend in the world yelled at me one day and said she had waited for me for the last time. She was so mad that I thought I had lost my best friend. That was the final straw; I'd had enough and decided that I was not going to be late any more. I set all of my clocks ahead 10 minutes and some of them I set ahead 15 minutes. Even though I knew they were set ahead 10 to 15 minutes later than it was, it worked. It seemed to be like a miracle.

It has been many years since I started this technique and to this day I am always known as the person who is early or on time. You would think that since you know that the clocks are set ahead of time that you would start to ignore it but, if you really want to change it will work. When you look up at the clock and you notice that it's time to go, you will get going.

Embrace Being Early

If being early feels like a waste of time, come prepared for the pause: bring a book or something to work on. Listen to a podcast or just closely notice the world around you. I have come to enjoy this time, catching up on a good book or TED talk. I even take time to write when I find I have a few extra minutes.

I hope my technique works as well for you as it has for me.

Marian LaSalle is an expert on networking, building and expanding business, podcasting, Internet marketing, and having fun. You can connect with her at http://www.MarianLaSalle.com.

Chapter 11
Late in Italy

by Maria Lassila

Late – not a word that I ever wanted to have associated with my name! I grew up with a parent who was always extremely late – it was not uncommon for her to arrive to pick me up hours after the appointed time. Since we were living in the Seattle area with its famous weather, I claimed the Genesis hit "Misunderstanding" as my theme song - "I waited in the rain for hours, you were late."

As an adult, I still consider being late a major pet peeve. So what was I thinking when I decided to move to Italy, not a country known for its punctuality? Well, I guess it didn't occur to me until I arrived that I was going to have to accept that things really ARE different here. For example, when attending an event, I've learned that posted start times are usually optimistic by at least 15 minutes. If I arrive on time, I'll have plenty of time to peruse the program and study the architecture of the venue. Specified durations of individual segments can be assumed to be suggested minimums. They are often prefaced by " I'll keep my remarks brief to stay within my allotted time" before being blithely ignored. Posted end times are pretty much irrelevant, other than to give cover to those who decide to leave "early" at the scheduled hour. Of course, if I ask others their opinions afterwards, most will mention that it would have been nice if the organizers could have managed the time better.

Now, even having lived in Milan for more than a decade, I still shake my head. Here in Italy it is commonly accepted that last-minute issues will come up. You might argue that when "unforeseen" delays are the rule rather than the exception that it's time to re-examine the rule. But it's never the fault of the person for being late – there was an abnormal amount of traffic, an unexpected visitor or phone call - or both – arrived at the very last moment, a family member needed to be attended to. And of course points have to be awarded for heroism that these last-minute obstacles were overcome at all with such a minor delay, rather than cancelling altogether.

A friend of mine loves regaling me with her tales of arriving at the very last minute for flights and trains – running from bus stops or taxis to the airport or train station where she lands in her seat moments before the doors are locked, gasping for breath and snickering with pride at having managed once more to cheat the clock. Running late makes me feel anxious - my stress level goes up just listening to her stories. I, on the other hand, leave plenty of time for unexpected delays. My Kindle and smartphone stowed in my handbag, I expect to have plenty of time to catch up on reading in the waiting room and I usually do. On the one occasion that I was stuck in an incredibly long airport security line, I was mortified to hear my name being announced over the airport public address system as I raced for the gate, convinced that I was going to be left behind. That was enough of a lesson learned, never again!

Why else do I avoid being late? Even when there's no scheduled departure involved, I make it a point to arrive when I've said I would. Not showing up as promised sends the message to others that I don't respect the value of their time – my agenda is more important and they should certainly understand. I feel I've let the other person down if I don't follow through on being there when I should. When something doesn't go as planned, I want to have the time to make adjustments, not be stuck making excuses for why the situation could have been better "if only." If something goes wrong, I won't have time to fix it and this will reflect badly on me, at least from my perspective. And of course I want to appear calm and collected, not harried and rushed. If I've made a commitment to be somewhere, I will have invested the time and energy to prepare for the presentation/conversation/celebration. Not showing up when agreed only detracts from the final effect – instead of entering confidently, I'll be spending some social capital on apologizing.

What do I do to avoid being late? Creating and using checklists is my favorite strategy. A few days before the event/appointment/departure, I start making a list of 1) things I need to take with me and 2) last-minute tasks that need to be completed (printing final versions, taxi reservation, etc). The day before, I place my checklist in a prominent spot – usually the side of my desk – where I will be able to see it and refer to it without searching for it. I begin building a stack of the items that I'll be taking – also in plain view – checking off each item from the list as I go along. I glance at the list every so often during the day to review my progress. I save copies of checklists on my computer – or better, in Dropbox, to always have them with me. That way I can use previous lists as templates for starting new ones, quickly reminding myself of vital items and steps to include.

What else do I do to avoid being late? It took me a long time to be able to do it and I still have to grit my teeth, but I stop checking my email at least half an hour before the time I need to depart. When I've broken this rule and peeked, it was pretty much guaranteed that there would be something that would only take a minute to address. But of course it would take much longer and before I knew it I would be looking at the clock – gnashing my teeth and cursing my weakness.

Probably the most important thing I've learned is that while I can control my own actions, I will never be able to control those of others. I maintain my own standards and punctuality is one of which I am proud. But I resign myself to the fact that the culture of my current chosen home will never come around to my ingrained Anglo point of view: that being late is the exception, not the rule to follow.

Maria Lassila is an online visibility strategist, podcast host, author and networking maven living in Milan, Italy, for more than a decade since her transplant from the west coast of the U.S. (Washington state and then Southern California). For 20 years she worked in the apparel industry, ranging from retail sales to managing production for luxury brands in ladies' shoes and golfwear. Her current focus is on helping small businesses and independent professionals grow their visibility with the English-speaking community in Milan, both online and off. Read more at

http://DoingBusinessInMilan.com

Chapter 12
Forever 10 Minutes Late
by Dr. Jeanette Cates

I am traditionally 10 minutes late. My friends know it. My family knows it. I readily admit it. That's why I found it ironic when Leslie asked me to contribute to this book. After all, what can a perennial late-comer share about being on time?

Upon reflection, I realized that I have not always been late. And I am not late for everything. That combination tells me that I *choose* to be late in certain situations.

If you struggle with being on time, these tips may help you isolate the when and why of being late. Once you do that, you can choose to be late - not.

When Are You Late?

Take a look at your life over the past week. When were you late? Are there certain types of activities for which you are always delayed? How late are you?

When I did this I found that I am generally 10 minutes late for personal appointments. When I worked in an office, I was also late coming into the office or coming back from lunch. Those two activities are predictable and consistent for me when it comes to "lateness."

On the other hand, I am **never** late for presentations, whether they are in person or online. I do a lot of online presentations (teleseminars and webinars) but I can count on one hand the number of times I've arrived "just in time" over the past ten years. I am generally online and ready for the presentation at least 10 minutes early.

To understand why there is such a difference, I had to ask myself the next question.

Is There A Reason To Be Late?

I didn't grow up being late. In fact, it was quite the opposite. While still in elementary school I fell in love with the story of "Cheaper by the Dozen." In the story, the father was an efficiency expert who valued time and effort. I loved the idea of saving even a second of time or extra effort by redesigning the way we do things!

By fifth grade I was creating "factories" and measuring the efficiency of the process. If we were assembling handouts in the classroom, I was the one who arranged them to most effectively collate and staple them with minimal movements. Yes, time and efficiency were that important to me!

I also grew up as a military child. Our household ran on time. When you attended an event, you were always there slightly before it started because you didn't dare arrive late. It just "was not done!"

I married a military man and again everything ran on time. All through my 20's I don't remember being late. Although I was a stay-at-home wife I was also active in community activities and always arrived on time.

So what changed? I entered the workplace! It became clear to me almost immediately that my fellow employees did not walk in, sit down and immediately get to work. Instead, they came in, had a cup of coffee, talked for a while, then ambled over to their desks. It drove me nuts!

As a young mother with a full-time job, I had more than enough to keep me busy. So the idea of wasting time each morning at work seemed like a bad idea. I determined that if my fellow workers were not going to actually get to work until 8:15 there was no reason for me to arrive at 8. After all, I didn't drink coffee and wasn't much of a socializer. And I could better use those 10-15 minutes on errands or short tasks that I needed to do personally. So I started coming in about 10 minutes late.

On the other hand, since I value time so highly, I would not think of being late for a presentation. As the presenter I don't want to waste the attendees' time. I want to start on time to honor their commitment to show up on time. Since I am the one controlling the time, I know that no time will be wasted. Therefore, I am never late when I am in charge.

What about you? You have already determined the situations in which you are late. Can you now identify what might trigger those times when you are late versus those times you are on time?

Watch Those Habits!

It's easy to fall into habits. You are late to lunch with a friend. She understands because she's gotten caught up at work herself. So you tell yourself it's okay.

The next time you meet for lunch, you decide to squeeze in one more email reply before you leave the office. Oops, you're about the same 10 minutes late. She's kept busy reading email while waiting for you. It's okay because she's not upset. And you did get that extra email finished!

That's how it starts. It's an innocent repetition that quickly turns into a habit. Soon you find yourself being 10 minutes late for everything!

Have you formed a bad habit of being late? Identify your patterns and decide whether or not you want to change the habit. Are you ready to change it or are you willing to accept it? If you choose not to change it, you may as well accept it and relax. Otherwise, you are putting an undue amount of stress on yourself!

Turn Off The Snooze Button

Your mind is very powerful. It has the ability to wake you up when you choose to wake up. It also has the power to tell you when you need to get up out of your chair and head out the door in order to arrive on time.

The problem is, we don't listen to our mind. We argue "just five more minutes." You hit the snooze button (physically or mentally) and roll over to grab a few more winks - or finish that email. I even know people who let the snooze button repeat 5, 6, 10 times! They could have gotten an extra hour of solid, uninterrupted sleep had they just decided to get up the first time the alarm sounded.

The same thing happens when you're trying to be on time. When you decide to be on time, you will be on time.

There Is No Try

Yoda tells us in the movie Star Wars to "Do or do not. There is no try." The same attitude can be applied to being on time.

You are not perfect. None of us are! If you determine that you have a habit of being late in certain situations, but are unwilling to change it, then accept it. Warn people that you are typically late. Let them know you won't be upset with them if *they* are late.

On the other hand, if you are truly serious about changing that habit, then make the decision to do something about it. Don't fall into the Snooze Button trap and think you have to set multiple alarms and warning. If you are decided about making the change, you can do it with the next appointment on your calendar.

Change is a decision, made in the moment. Breaking the habit takes time. Stick with it and in just a few weeks you will be able to say "I am always on time!"

Dr. Jeanette Cates is an author and Internet strategist. She is known for saving time and being organized. Jeanette shares her systems and tips in Organize Your Online Business and her newest book, Productivity Pointers. You can reach Jeanette on social media and her website at JeanetteCates.com

Chapter 13
Would People Mistake You For The White Rabbit in <u>Alice in Wonderland</u>?

by Cynthia Charleen Alexander

Would people mistake you for the White Rabbit in Alice in Wonderland who says, "I'm late! I'm late, for a very important date. No time to say 'Hello, Goodbye.' I'm late, I'm late, I'm late!"

Would you rather be known as the person who is punctual, instead? Do you remember in school when tardiness meant a trip by the office to get a permission slip for class? There was a reason for this – to train us to be timely.

The Rolling Stones sang about it with their lyrics "Time, time, time is on my side. Yes it is." Well, I have news for Mick: "Time and tide wait for no man." according to Geoffrey Chaucer.

All that being said, being on time is an important habit to establish.

Since we can't add time to our days, let's make our days more efficient and make the best use of what we have available.

Let's review how a day typically starts:

- The alarm sounds – do you hop out of bed or hit the snooze and continue dreaming?
- What time is it when your alarm goes off?
- First steps – where do they lead – to the computer or the kitchen?
- Breakfast – do you eat a healthy one or just grab a cup of coffee and some cereal? (Or, not even cereal?)
- What does your morning routine resemble – a finely tuned machine or a runaway tractor?

Here are some tips on getting going fast – and keeping up the momentum throughout the morning. I think we can agree that using less time to get ready can add time to your morning and get you to work – on time! What if your day started like this:

- Alarm sounds and your eyes open to quiet, uncluttered surroundings. You are refreshed and ready to face the day.
- You smell the aroma of coffee and know you have prepared a bit of breakfast last night before you went to bed?

A few tips about breakfast:

Decide what you will have before going to bed the night before. Also, if you are not a big breakfast eater, or if you want to have a quick breakfast, make a protein shake first thing in the morning. If you have a good blender, then breakfast can be quick and easy. Keep the ingredients close to where you will make the shake.

When you open the refrigerator, have the basic ingredients grouped together where they are easy to reach. Flax seed, kale, nuts and cinnamon are ingredients that are contained in many recipes for shakes. Take a couple of minutes to sit and enjoy breakfast before resuming your new routine.

Are you a big breakfast person? Try preparing some of the dishes at the beginning of the week so you only need to heat things such as bacon or sausage while you scramble that egg. You can keep things in easy to use containers so time can be saved, even in small ways.

Next on the agenda is getting ready for work or school. When you get to the bathroom, everything should be ready so you can make best use of the remaining minutes – it's get out the door on time day!

Baskets, drawers, even small buckets can be used to keep the essentials ready for use. Have a basic makeup routine that is easy to follow. It can be simplified by selecting products that multi-task. Makeup base can be combined with moisturizer and sun block. There is a compressed powder that combines a mineral powder with blocking capability. Moisturizing lipstick that has sunscreen is helpful, too.

Does this give you any ideas about where you can trim time off your routine?

You can go one step further, if you really get into the mood. How about a easy-care hairstyle? Have you tried putting out your clothes for the next day before going to bed? And speaking of clothes...how organized is your closet?

You would be surprised how much time can be saved by doing a little reorganization of the closets! If you are not organized now, it is costing you both time and money. Creating a wardrobe plan is one of my favorite ways to work with clients. One of the first things noticed is how a person looks. If your shoes are in good condition and clean, that is a good first step in meeting with a client.

If you have a jumble of clothes to choose from, you could streamline to some basic styles and colors. Pick a basic outfit for the next day. Co-ordinate with shoes and accessories and then take just a minute to look in the mirror and feel good about "the New You!"

Are you starting to detect a pattern in this preparation? You guessed it – analyze, strategize and then implement new ideas and habits.

Do you have children or students that interfere with your being punctual? The same technique will work for them. Sit down and work out a plan as a family and see where a bit of organizing can enable you to leave in a timely fashion.

Something as simple as a homework routine can clear lots of stress when it comes time to leave for school. If at the end of the day, all homework is done, notes signed, and all books and papers are in the backpack before going to bed, there will be a calmer exit in the morning.

The same principle applies to you and any work you need to take to the office or client. Have the work finished and ready to go out the door the next morning before going to bed. Do you have a last minute scramble to find your keys? Here is a tip that will work if you follow it...

If you carry a purse, use a model with pockets on the front or easily reached on the inside. Put your keys and phone there when you come home, instead of tossing them aside. Just this one simple change will clear some of the chaos as there will be no need for a search party to scout out where your keys landed last time they entered the room.

Everyone is going to run a bit behind schedule on occasion, however, doing so frequently can send the wrong signals to your boss (even if you are your own boss) as it can seem to be a lack of commitment to what needs to be done on a project or task.

Do you want to be noticed at work? Would you like to be chosen for a special assignment sometime? Prove you can handle small tasks well and bring your part of a project to completion. Having it done well and promptly, will show that you are ready to handle something important over time.

A simple plan for the morning routine can restore harmony to your morning and enable you to actually look forward to the day when that alarm sounds and you decide right then how your day will begin.

So in the words of Lord Chesterfield, "Take care of the minutes and the hours will take care of themselves."

Cynthia Charleen Alexander is an expert at organizing home offices for business owners. Learn more about her services and connect with her at
http://GetYourHomeOfficeOrganized.com.

Chapter 14
The Queen of Lists

by Adrienne Dupree

Adrienne Dupree is a lot of things, but one thing she is known for are her lists. I live and die by lists. These lists can either be a paper list, an electronic list, a spreadsheet or tasks entered into my phone. I am definitely a left brain person so this works for me. I usually have a million things all going on at once since I still have a full-time job as a Program Manager and I also have a part-time online marketing business. Having all of that going on at the same time can be very hectic and also overwhelming. The one thing that keeps it all together is my lists.

Don't Miss Your Flight

Currently, most of my travel is for conferences that I attend for my online marketing business. They are all out of town so I have to fly to attend. Usually there is a whirlwind of activity prior to the trip. It never fails that there is some deadline that needs be fulfilled at work when it is time for me to go out of town. I am typically up almost 24 hours prior to the trip, so I need to create a system that ensures that I will be on time for my flight and not forget anything. Also, I normally book a very early flight between 6 AM and 7AM which makes it even more imperative that I am organized so I do not miss my flight. Below are the things that I do to make sure I am on time for my flights.

I sign up for text messages and email so that I am notified of any changes with my flight. As you know, flight changes and delays are a part of flying.

I make a list a few days before the flight of all the things I need for the trip so I will not forget anything. I make sure to include cords on the list for any electronics that I plan to take. The last thing I want to do is try to find a place to buy a cord that I inadvertently left behind.

As I start packing my suitcase and computer bag, I cross things off the list. This allows me to keep track of the things that still need to be packed.

I try to pack most things the night before so I am not scrambling in the morning.

I check the weather the night before to determine if I need to leave earlier due to bad weather.

I always check in electronically24 hours in advance. I do not want to wait to the last minute to check in since most planes are overbooked these days.

I arrange a shuttle or cab back to the airport the day I arrive so I am not scrambling when it is time to leave. Usually for a shuttle, you get a break in price if you book roundtrip as opposed to one-way.

When it is time to return home, I pack my suitcase the night before. I also get my clothes ready that I will wear to the airport the night before as well.

I always use curbside check-in which usually has a shorter line than checking in at the counter. Some people may prefer to check in inside because you don't have leave a tip. Believe me, that tip is worth the convenience.

On my return trip, I typically get to the airport very early because I am not as familiar with the airport. You never know how long it will take to get through security.

Employing these tips leads to stress-free traveling.

The Front Row

When I go to live events, I usually arrive the day before. This gives me a chance to scope out the hotel and room where the conference will be held. I can find out where the closest restrooms are to the room as well as what eating places are convenient for lunch. Since I always have multiple electronics, I also like to check to see where the plugs are located. To ensure that I am on time for the event, I determine how long I need to get ready so I can set the alarm appropriately. I use my phone so that I can set multiple alarms or snooze times if necessary. Since I am a night-owl, it takes me some time to get moving in the morning. I get my clothes ready the night before so I can sleep later. I also determine what I need to carry to the event and pack it the night before as well.

Since I like to sit in the front of the room, I make sure that I arrive early for the event. The last thing I want to do is arrive late and then walk to the front of the room. I guess sitting in the front of the room dates back to when I was in school. I always liked to sit in the front of the room so I can see and hear what is going on. Also, usually the people that sit in the front are less likely to talk which is distracting to me. I will typically arrive 15 to 30 minutes before the event starts. Most of the time, I will put my things down and then go get some tea.

As you can see, I am pretty methodical about being on time for flights and live events. My routine may seem pretty anal to some but it works for me. Preparing in advance leads to less stress for me. I know that some people just wing it when it comes to travel as far as packing, but I believe that would lead to me forgetting things. We all have our pet peeves and you need to determine what works for you.

Adrienne Dupree is a full-time Program Manager for a government contractor and a part-time online marketer. She has a technical background with a B.S. Mathematics, B.S. Electrical Engineering and M.S. Computer Science. Her company, The Online Newbie, is for people in corporate America who want to get out the rat race, stop trading time for dollars and be in control of their own destiny so that they can start an online marketing business. To find out more about Adrienne Dupree and The Online Newbie and how you can leave the corporate world behind go to
http://www.theonlinenewbie.com .

Chapter 15
I Hate to Be Late:
I Am Finally Learning How to
Be On Time!

by Leslie Ann Cardinal

I am finally learning how to be on time! I am so happy to report to you that I am much more on time than ever before. And even though I am still late occasionally, I can usually see where I got off track or where the delay happened so that I can continue to improve. This is a very exciting accomplishment for me and I want to share with you some of the things that have worked best for me. My hope is that you will find encouragement and inspiration and strategies to help you be more on time too.

I have had challenges for many years with being late. It seemed like no matter how hard I tried I could not reliably count on being on time. It was very frustrating to me and hard on the people around me. I decided that I wanted to do something about it. My techniques and ideas for being on time just weren't working. I researched many time management books and online resources too, but I found very little that would help me to me be more on time.

So I decided to use an approach that has worked well for me in other areas of my life: I asked several of my friends and colleagues to share the methods that have helped them to be on time, with the hope that some of their techniques would work for me as well. They shared great ideas with me! (And if they were willing, I asked them to share their ideas by writing a short chapter for this book. I hope you will read each of their chapters so you can benefit from their wonderful encouragement, wisdom, and helpful strategies too.)

During the past twelve months, I have experimented with their ideas to see which ones would work best for me. Some of their suggestions helped me to develop a new mindset. Other suggestions guided me to develop new habits. In this chapter, I will share with you the key ideas that have made the biggest difference in my own journey to learn how to be on time. I invite you to try them out to find the ideas that may work well for you too.

Believe that it really is possible to be on time. Believe that it is possible to learn strategies and habits to help you with this. This was a mindset change that gradually grew stronger as I began to have success. If you have had many years of challenges with being late, this may be a big change in the way you see yourself and in what you believe is truly possible. I really want you to take hope from the ideas in this book and to believe that it is worth the effort to make changes.

Celebrate your successes and your progress. As you work with the techniques in this book, it could be that arriving five minutes late is actually big progress for you. That's great! Celebrate it! And look back to see what you did that helped you to accomplish that victory. This will help you to repeat your successful strategies. You may also see where you could adjust a little bit to get even closer to your goal of being on time. If it suits your personality, you may even want to track your results so you can clearly see your progress and celebrate often.

Shift your focus and go further "upstream" in your time planning. This was one of the first big changes for me. When I talked about this shift with my husband who is a naturally an on-time person, he just looked at me and said, "That's obvious!" But it wasn't obvious to me beforehand. When I really looked at how I was approaching the process of getting ready to leave for appointments, I found that my attention was focused on the actual time of the appointment. It seemed logical to me to focus on that point in time. But this didn't help me to get out the door early enough and I was often late.

So I started to experiment. Instead of focusing on the appointment time, I tried focusing on the time I needed to leave the house for the appointment. But even that wasn't very successful and I still found myself in a rush to leave and still I was often late. So I shifted my focus even earlier to the time when I needed to start to get ready. I found it was much sooner than I would have started getting ready when my focus was on the actual appointment time. After I made this shift, I finally began to be on time more often.

Allow for an extra margin of time. The next adjustment I started making was also one that my husband says was obvious. But again, it wasn't so obvious to me. I noticed that I was making my time plans based on arriving at the scheduled time of the appointment. But if any little glitch happened, like having to wait at a railroad crossing or extra heavy traffic, I could still end up being late. I didn't know how to manage this and still arrive at the time of the appointment. So I asked myself a more extreme question: Were there any situations when I was always on time, with time to spare?

When I asked this question, the best example I could think of is when I am going to the airport to take a flight. With airline travel, the recommendation is to arrive two hours before departure time for domestic flights. I have consistently been able to arrive on time for my flights, even though I may not make it a full two hours ahead of departure time. But by allowing for a lot of "margin," I am still on time, with time to wait before the flight leaves.

But arriving two hours early is such an extreme amount of extra time that it doesn't seem like a practical strategy for my everyday appointments. But this got me to thinking more about the idea of allowing for a "margin" of extra time before the appointment, rather than trying to arrive exactly on time. I wondered how much extra time I should work into my time plan, so I could be on time and never (or almost never) late?

This led to my next experiment which is to aim to arrive ten to fifteen minutes early rather than right on time. Even now, this still doesn't feel completely normal and comfortable for me yet. It means starting to get ready to leave at a much earlier time than I would have in the past. I am still adjusting to this thought process and working to establish this as a new habit in my life. I find that it takes a real effort of will to stop whatever I am doing at that time and to switch gears into getting ready to leave. But when I do, I am usually rewarded with being on time, and that feels good! But it led to the next challenge too.

Plan creatively for the waiting time and the travel time. I must confess that I have felt some resistance to planning for more waiting time. Allowing more time to get ready, allowing more time for travel, and on top of that, allowing for a "margin" of waiting time when I arrived, seemed like a really big chunk of time. Planning this much time felt hard to manage with everything that was on my daily "To Do" list. So I experimented with two strategies to address this. The easiest strategy is to plan for a few ways that I could use these blocks of time. For travel time, I listen to excellent audio books and podcasts. I think of my car as my rolling "university" where I can continually grow my business knowledge.

For waiting time at the place of an appointment, I want productive ways to use the waiting time, so that it doesn't feel like I am wasting time. If it is a networking meeting or a family gathering, being a little early means extra time to build relationships or to offer to help with preparations. For other situations, waiting time became an opportunity for a quick stop in the restroom to freshen up, checking voicemail or email, praying, writing, reading, listening to books and podcasts, and even planning future projects.

Aim for progress, not immediate perfection. This is an important idea. As you experiment with these techniques, you will need to make adjustments to make them fit you. For example, you'll need to experiment to see how much time you actually need to get dressed and ready to leave for appointments. You may need to adjust for the amount of time needed in the early morning compared to the amount of time needed in the afternoon or the evening. Just notice and continue to adjust to personalize your system for yourself and your family. It may take a bit of trial and error to find the right combination for you.

Be realistic in your expectations. Don't expect 100% perfection right away. You may still be late sometimes. Just notice what works and what doesn't. Forgive yourself when you are late and aim to do better the next time. Apologize if you are late and aim for ongoing improvement as you work towards being more and more on time.

Avoid predictable time problems such as searching for your car keys or your cell phone. Choose a place in your home to designate as a "launch pad" for things that you will need to take with you when you leave for appointments. This is especially important for things like your car keys, but it can also include your phone, purse or briefcase, papers, backpack, and umbrella. Use a sticky note to remind you about anything that might be in the fridge or in a closet that needs to go out the door with you too.

Do your best to keep your vehicle in good repair. Manage your laundry schedule so that you always have a change of clothes in case you spill something at the last minute and need to change. Check your gas level the day before to ensure you have plenty of fuel to reach your destination without having to make a quick stop for gas the next day.

Minimize distractions as you get ready to leave. I noticed that one of my biggest challenges with being on time is that I can easily get distracted when I need to be getting ready to leave. The newspaper, the cats, the dishes, the mail, and many other things are right there on my path and can easily catch my attention. And once that happens, it can put me five minutes, ten minutes, or even 30 minutes behind my planned schedule.

As you get ready for appointments, know what kinds of things distract you. Then look ways to avoid or minimize those distractions. For example, it is often better if I get right into the shower when I get up, without going to the kitchen to make my morning cup of tea first. There are many distractions in the kitchen area. By getting into the shower first, I am already making progress on the steps to getting ready and I seem to have better success with being on time when I do that.

Consider partnering with your spouse or family members, but only if they are positive and supportive. If you have family members who are good at being on time, you may want to ask them to work with you and help you. For example, I often ask my husband what time he thinks we should be ready to walk out the door for an appointment. I compare his answer with what my own answer would have been. I also ask him how he determined his answer so I can learn from his thought process. He knows that I sincerely want to be better at being on time, so he doesn't give me a sarcastic answer. This has helped me a lot and I think he appreciates my efforts and my respect for his opinion.

Time yourself to see how long it takes you to get ready. This could include tasks like showering, doing hair and makeup or shaving, taking care of pets, getting coffee, preparing and eating breakfast, getting your vehicle loaded up or cleared of ice and snow, and packing a lunch. Write down each task and the amount of time it generally requires. This will help you to make a realistic plan and schedule for getting ready and getting out the door.

You may also want to think about which of these tasks could be done beforehand. Some things could be done the day or the evening before. Or, there may be tasks that can be streamlined to shorten the amount of time needed. You may even be able to eliminate some steps altogether to help you be on time.

Keep a clock visible as you get ready. A wall clock or an alarm clock works well. The important thing is to have it be right in your line of sight. This can help you to minimize distractions and to help you to stay aware of the current time so you can keep focused on getting ready to leave on time.

Use scouting runs and repeatable routines. If you are going somewhere new for an important appointment, you may find it helpful to do a scouting run. Drive to the location the day beforehand, or even earlier. This will help you to find the exact location, to see the route to take, and to locate the best place to park. This strategy is especially important when you are in a different city, but it works well at home too, when you are going downtown or to an area that is not as familiar to you.

For places or appointment you travel to regularly, develop a routine that you can repeat each time to help you be on time. An example of this is going to a series of medical appointments, or going to sporting events for home games. A routine helps you know where to go, where to park, where to enter the building, and how much time you will need for the whole process.

Claim the benefits of being on time. As I have been more on time, I notice that I feel calmer and happier and more relaxed when I am preparing for appointments. This means less stress, less adrenaline, and not feeling as rushed. This seems to translate into more energy to bring to my projects and appointments and relationships. This is good for everyone involved.

Notice how good it feels to be on time. Enjoy the feeling of being more relaxed and confident about having enough time for travel and a few minutes to wait before your appointments. Your progress can help the people around you to feel more calm and relaxed too. Relish the good feelings. You may even want to give yourself little rewards to celebrate your progress.

In Conclusion

I believe in you! You really can be on time more often. Be creative, try the techniques. Be willing to experiment and adjust them so that they work for you and your family. And, as your life and your circumstances change, continue to modify and adjust them again, if necessary.

Ultimately, it will be up to you to find ways to be successfully on time. I hope that the ideas in this book will give you a strong feeling of hope as well as lots of specific positive ideas that will help you every day. Read this book with a highlighter or a pen and mark the ideas that you think will work best for you. Every chapter in this book offers a wonderful variety of techniques as the authors share their stories to offer you help and encouragement.

I wish you great success and lots of joy and satisfaction as you work toward the goal of being on time. Thank you for reading this book. I look forward to hearing your story of success soon!

Appendix

10 Great Benefits to Being on Time

If you struggle with being on time, it can feel like a huge challenge to be on time. You may wonder if it is really possible or if it is worth the effort when it seems so difficult to accomplish. Sometimes all you can see is the pain or discomfort of being late that you would really like to avoid. A powerful element to helping you to achieve your goal of being on time can be to get really clear about the great benefits of being on time. Use these positive benefits to help pull yourself forward as you establish this new habit of being on time. Here are some of the wonderful benefits you may experience that can make it truly worth the effort to learn how to be more on time.

1. Being on time feels like a real victory, especially when you are first developing this new habit. Those good feelings can help to reinforce all the effort and thought you are putting into being on time.

2. Being on time is much less stressful on your body, because there is much less adrenaline is flowing when you are on time. This will likely be good for your health, and perhaps also for the health of the other people who are affected by your being on time.

3.   Being on time boosts your self-esteem and your self-confidence every time you are successful in being on time. And I believe strong positive self-esteem and self-confidence help you achieve other goals that are important to you too.

4.   Being on time allows you to be present when events start. By being on time you won't miss important announcements or introductions or overviews that happen at the beginning of events. You may even save money and time by avoiding the need to reschedule appointments because of being too late.

5.   Being on time helps to keep you in a positive frame of mind rather than anxious or upset or tense as you are getting ready and as you travel to appointments.

6.   Being on time builds or maintains other people's positive perception of you as a person who is dependable and reliably on time. This can flow over into their positive opinion about you in other areas too.

7.   Being on time frees up your thoughts and energy to focus on the appointment or the event or the meeting, helping you to bring your creativity and resourcefulness and experience to the situation.

8.   Being on time reduces "friction" or negative feelings in your relationships. Being on time

helps to minimize feelings of anger or hurt or annoyance that can happen when you are late. It helps to keep your relationships in good shape.

9.   Being on time allows you to move forward toward your goals, rather than potentially getting stuck and bogged down with possible concerns about other people's possible negative reactions if you were late.

10.   Being on time will help to build and sustain your wonderful new identity as a person who is almost always on time. This will feel really good to you and to the people around you. It really is worth the effort to build this new habit!

10 Mistakes to Avoid When You Want to be On Time

When you really want to be on time, there are several common challenges that can make you late almost every time. See if you have a few of these challenges that are affecting your ability to be on time. This list comes from my own experiences and I have worked to develop solutions for each one. I invite you to try the suggested solutions, or to create your own solutions that will work well for you.

1. Trying to do just one more thing before you leave for an appointment.

Suggested Solution: Make a note of the task on your daily "To Do" list so you'll remember it and then do the task at a later time. It can almost always wait until later. It's so tempting to think that it will only take a minute, but taking time to do that one task can easily make the difference between being on time and being late.

2. Answering the telephone when you are in the process of getting ready to leave for an appointment.

Suggested Solution: Let the call go to voicemail. Even though it seems like it would just take a minute to answer, it is too easy to get caught up in a conversation and your focus on getting ready will be disrupted. Voicemail is your friend in this situation because it will take the message and allow you to respond when you have more time. If you arrive at your destination early, you may have the option to check voicemail and to return the call.

3. Hoping that there won't be much traffic if you are driving to an appointment.

Suggested Solution: Allow extra time because there may actually be extra traffic or construction or even an accident. Check your maps or GPS at least the day before to be sure you know the route. If you aren't familiar with the route, consider driving it a few days before your appointment to be sure you know exactly where to go.

4. Speeding on the way to an appointment to try to get to your destination faster.

Suggested Solution: Drive at a safe speed within the speed limit. This will help you to arrive safely. It will also help to reduce the risk of being late because of getting a speeding ticket, not to mention the expense and the impact on your insurance.

5. Doing grooming tasks like shaving or putting on makeup in your car as you drive.

Suggested Solution: The best solution is to do those personal grooming tasks at home. Second option is to bring the items with you to use at your destination if you arrive a bit early. Please don't put yourself and other drivers at risk by trying to do these tasks while you are driving.

6. Thinking it will take less time than usual to do the steps in your "getting ready" routine.

Suggested Solution: Time yourself to see how much time it takes to do the various steps in your routine. Allow extra time if you are tired or if you are travelling or have other variations in your situation. As a bonus suggestion, look at your routine to see if there are some steps you can eliminate or streamline in some way to reduce the time you need to get ready.

7. Thinking there won't be interruptions as you get ready, if you have other people around you.

Suggested Solution: Think ahead about how you can prevent or handle interruptions. With family members, you may want to have an agreement about everyone staying focused while getting ready. You will benefit from having a night-before routine. You may find it helpful to get up earlier in the morning than the rest of the family so that you can have some quiet, uninterrupted time to get ready for your day.

8. Packing the same day that you are leaving for a trip.

Suggested Solution: When you are preparing for a trip, pack the day before, or even sooner if possible. About a week ahead of time, make a checklist of preparation tasks and things to pack. This will let you work in those extra tasks into your days before the trip.

9. Not keeping enough gas in your car, or waiting until the morning of your appointment to put gas in your car.

Suggested Solution: Set a standard for yourself about the amount of gas you keep in your car at all times. I recommend not letting the level go below a quarter of a tank (keep more in the tank during winter). If you have an appointment in the morning, fill the tank no later than the night before so you don't have the rush and risk of a delay in the morning.

   10. Not having a "staging area" where you can put items you need to take with you.

   Suggested Solution: Choose an area in your home where you can put items you need to remember to take with you when you leave. Have a specific designated place for this and have everyone in the household use it. Items to place in the staging area could include backpacks, briefcase, lunch, water bottle, snacks, purse, keys, jacket, glasses, phone, laptop, umbrella, and papers or folders. Have a specific place where you put your keys when you arrive home so that you always know where they are.

10 Things You Can Do When You Arrive Early

Hooray! You are arriving early to your appointments more and more often. That's great! When I started to focus on being on time more often, one of my concerns was about what I would do if I was early. I didn't want to go in to the appointment too early. That can be as annoying to people as being late. And I didn't want to just sit and wait. That felt like wasted time. So I began to make a list of ideas for ways to use the time well when I was early. Here are some of the ideas from the list that may work for you, too.

1. Check voicemails.

2. Make short phone calls, if you are in a place where you will not disturb other people.

3. Write. This can include articles, work on a book, blog posts, notes for a talk, email messages, greeting cards, or thank you notes.

4. Bring a book or a magazine to read. Or read on your Kindle or other device.

5. Listen to podcasts, the radio, or audiobooks.

6. Relax or meditate or pray for a few minutes. Take some deep breaths to be calm and centered.

7. Do some people-watching.

8. Eat a light snack.

9. Connect with people on social media.

10. Outline a project, or brainstorm for ideas.

About the Author

Leslie Ann Cardinal is a Professional Certified Coach who works with entrepreneurs to make rapid progress toward their goals. She has more than 25 years of experience working with leaders and business owners in many industries. She brings her unique background of Industrial Engineering, Leadership Development, and a deep knowledge of how adults learn and achieve success. Learn more by visiting www.GrowYourBusinessNow.com.

Please be sure to claim your free resources related to this book at http://IHateToBeLate.com .

I would love to encourage you as you pursue your dreams and goals. Let's connect online:

http://GrowYourBusinessNow.com
Facebook.com/LeslieCardinal
LinkedIn.com/in/LeslieCardinal
Twitter.com/LeslieCardinal
Podcast on iTunes: Grow Your Business Now

www.ingramcontent.com/pod-product-compliance
Lightning Source LLC
Chambersburg PA
CBHW060618210326
41520CB00010B/1387